**I Deliver
Parcels
in Beijing**

I Deliver Parcels in Beijing

On Making a Living

Hu Anyan

ALLEN LANE
an imprint of
PENGUIN BOOKS

ALLEN LANE

UK | USA | Canada | Ireland | Australia
India | New Zealand | South Africa

Allen Lane is part of the Penguin Random House group of companies whose addresses can be found at global.penguinrandomhouse.com.

Penguin Random House UK
One Embassy Gardens, 8 Viaduct Gardens, London SW11 7BW

penguin.co.uk

Originally published as *Wo Zai Beijing Song Kuadi* by Shanghai Insight Media Co., Ltd
This translation first published in the United States by Astra Publishing House 2025
First published in Great Britain by Allen Lane 2025
005

Copyright © Hu Anyan, 2022
Translation copyright © Jack Hargreaves, 2025

The moral right of the author has been asserted

Penguin Random House values and supports copyright.
Copyright fuels creativity, encourages diverse voices, promotes freedom of expression and supports a vibrant culture. Thank you for purchasing an authorized edition of this book and for respecting intellectual property laws by not reproducing, scanning or distributing any part of it by any means without permission. You are supporting authors and enabling Penguin Random House to continue to publish books for everyone.
No part of this book may be used or reproduced in any manner for the purpose of training artificial intelligence technologies or systems. In accordance with Article 4(3) of the DSM Directive 2019/790, Penguin Random House expressly reserves this work from the text and data mining exception.

Printed and bound in Great Britain by Clays Ltd, Elcograf S.p.A.

The authorized representative in the EEA is Penguin Random House Ireland, Morrison Chambers, 32 Nassau Street, Dublin D02 YH68

A CIP catalogue record for this book is available from the British Library

ISBN: 978–0–241–73382–0

Penguin Random House is committed to a sustainable future for our business, our readers and our planet. This book is made from Forest Stewardship Council® certified paper.

Contents

Translator's Note — xi

I
My Year of Night Shifts in a Logistics Warehouse — 1

II
I Deliver Parcels in Beijing — 32

III
Odd Jobs in Shanghai — 155

IV
Other Jobs I've Had — 189

V
Other Sides of Life — 312

I Deliver Parcels in Beijing

Translator's Note

"Hard work" can mean many different things. A job might be technically or physically hard to do. One can work hard at something—to learn a skill, to improve in a certain way, or to make amends. A colleague might feel a lot like hard work. Hu Anyan shares his own experiences with all kinds of hard work in his candid, searching memoir, which traces his changing relationship to labor and creativity, as he learns how to make space for both to coexist in his life. The struggles and realizations he has along the way feel familiar to me as a translator, despite my work being a far cry from that of a delivery guy or parcel sorter.

I'd like to briefly explain a few aspects of this translated text, to give some insight into why this version of Hu's memoir reads the way it does. This translation is based on one Mandarin Chinese version of the book—there are a few in total—and includes short passages written exclusively for the English publication. Any other slight deviations from the Chinese editions are the result of editorial choices made in the interest of rhythmic and narrative flow.

A term that is repeated in the book and does not really evoke in English an accurate idea of the city spaces that comprise

Hu's delivery rounds is "neighborhood." These residential developments, known in Chinese as *xiaoqu* (lit. "small district"), are walled, often gated communities that contain groups of six-story walk-ups or, in newer complexes, possibly tens of high-rise apartment buildings each housing thousands of people. These neighborhoods sometimes verge on being separate ecosystems, with little gardens, playgrounds and schools for children, stores and restaurants, clinics.

Here I will address the system of naming that I used for them in the book, if I can call it a "system" at all, since the approach is fairly unscientific and inconsistent. Any of the neighborhoods, with an existing English translation I could locate online, are given those same names here. For the rest, I had three considerations in mind: 1) readers unfamiliar with Chinese might struggle to parse and pronounce long strands or dense clusters of pinyin, the official phonetic romanization for Chinese characters; 2) keeping some remnant of the Chinese names in the English translations should create a stronger sense of place than otherwise and also means that readers who know Chinese and, in particular know Beijing well, might be able to better situate the story; 3) the language of real estate can be quite bombastic and ostentatious when it wants to be, so why shouldn't these translations be, too? I hope the names based on these considerations will feel authentic and realistic to readers.

1

My Year of Night Shifts in a Logistics Warehouse

I say a year, but really, I was at D Company for just over ten months. I joined on May 12, on the ninth anniversary of the Wenchuan earthquake. My job was package handler at a hub in Shunde District, in Foshan, which at the time was the largest distribution center in the country. I only learned this after I left. Though the scale shocked me while I was there, I never really cared where the warehouse ranked nationally.

The distribution center was in a logistics park along with centers for JD.com, Vipshop, and BEST Express. I worked the night shift, from seven in the evening until seven the next morning. I had four days off a month. Almost everyone there worked nights, since sorting didn't happen during the day. The basic requirement for the job was to be able to read the addresses on labels. Nobody ever asked to see my diploma, but for sure there were people from back home that this would have disqualified.

The interview was a mere formality; the reality was they wouldn't turn anyone away who was willing to complete a three-day unpaid trial. This must have violated labor laws, but I asked around and apparently all the enterprises in the logistics park operated the same way. If you couldn't accept it, you had to look for work elsewhere.

Practically speaking, the trial was kind of necessary. A lot of first timers would otherwise not have known where to start. It was a chance for employer and employee to come to a mutual understanding. So far as I could tell, it also tended to cut numbers by more than half. Some people stuck it out for barely two hours before giving up. So, the least the company could have done was compensate anyone who still reported for duty after those three days.

The company wasn't devoid of humanity, though: Many people who moved to the area specially for work brought very little with them, so the employer made sure to grant half a month's salary at the end of the first twenty days for them to buy essentials. Otherwise, payday wasn't until the fifteenth of the following month.

The transfer center resembled a large pier. We worked on a yard-high cement platform, which we called the sorting floor. It was the length of eight, maybe ten, soccer fields and had an enormous steel roof overhead. All along both sides of it, there were loading and unloading docks, each of them numbered, and row upon row of trucks parked with their rears to the platform and their cargo doors open. I was welcomed onto the sorting floor each evening by a constant rumbling sound, low and heavy, like distant thunder: the sound of a hundred-plus forklifts rolling across the ground in unison. These forklifts were like worker ants unloading huge sacks of packages from trucks for delivery to the various sorting teams and carrying the sorted cargo to the corresponding loading dock.

I was assigned to a "small items" team, whose job it was to sort and repack parcels, as they arrived, according to destination. I mostly enjoyed the work: There was no need for talking, no need to use my brain, I just rolled up my sleeves and got on with it.

Since this was Guangdong, summer lasted for three-quarters of the year. In the day, the sun baked down on the metal roof until it was scorching hot, and the evenings were not that much cooler. Often, sweat was dripping down my back within the first two hours of a shift and would not stop dripping until the next morning. I eventually bought a three-liter flask for water that I finished every night, but I sweated so much I never once needed to pee while on shift.

For my trial I was put on unpacking, the most tiring of the roles. The parcels sent over from the service point arrived in large polypropylene bags that it was our team's task to open and empty onto the sorting floor, where we organized and rebagged them. Unpacking was the tearing-the-bags-open-and-tipping-out-the-contents part. The bags varied in weight, with some parcels weighing only several pounds, and the heaviest up to ten times that. If our shifts had been shorter, then I'm sure most people could have coped, but at the end of the night we all eventually started to lag; this was why unpacking was the one job that women weren't allowed to do.

In fact, it was a compulsory part of the training for every man, whereas the women went straight to repacking. It was only by going through the toughest tasks that the company and the candidate could know with enough certainty whether they were a good match, and therefore reduce the likelihood of "breaking up" over a misunderstanding later. Those few days of the trial period really were the hardest, since the body hadn't adjusted to the new work and its intensity yet. Unfamiliar movement causes extra fatigue anyway, which was partly why so many people called it after only a couple hours. But if you could hang in there long enough, eventually the workload would start to feel more manageable.

I remember an older woman during her trial, she seemed to have no problem with the toil, but left suddenly at midnight. I heard later that she couldn't read, so the foreman had talked her into quitting. She can't have been illiterate, I don't think, otherwise she wouldn't have managed those first hours without a mistake. She must have recognized some characters and asked team members for help with the rest, which will have put enough fear into her teammates that they decided to tell the foreman. She only had to mislabel one bag and all those parcels would have been sent to the wrong city, and everybody in the team would have had money docked from their pay.

We worked twelve hours every day, with a half-hour break for dinner, starting from nine, after we'd been there for two hours already. Then from ten in the evening until five in the morning was nonstop grind, followed by the slower final couple hours of the shift.

The yard had two canteens run by two different contractors, each selling different styles of food. We spooned out the dishes ourselves, like it was self-service, and paid according to weight. But there was unlimited free rice. Anyone wanting to save money filled up on bowls of it and had only a little of the other dishes. The prices were reasonable, in all fairness, and the canteens were mostly clean. After eating, we worked nine and a half hours altogether without a snack break. Some people brought in their own bread or crackers and scarfed them in a spare moment around midnight. Others had gotten used to not eating at all for ten hours straight. I would take in crackers myself, and on the days I forgot to, I could hear my stomach grumble.

I remember my first night there. No one told me the schedule, so I had dinner before turning up. When nine o'clock came around and everybody went to eat, I had no appetite and skipped the chance for a substantial meal, assuming there would be food later on. Little did I know I'd have to keep going for the next half night with only water to fuel me. By the end of the shift, I was so hungry my head was spinning. Weight loss was par for the course for new workers. I had one colleague who joined a few days after me and dropped from 180 pounds to 130 in only three months. I wasn't exactly fat before starting, but some months in I'd lost a dozen pounds.

I soon discovered that most people who worked there weren't big talkers or there to make friends. They reminded me of quiet old farmers—even if they weren't very old—they just had the same indifferent, guarded way about them with strangers. Happily, I'm not a fan of chitchat either, so everyone working with their mouths shut was fine by me, I felt comfortable in that environment. But when I asked for guidance, they always giggled shyly before awkwardly giving an answer—they weren't arrogant though, just quiet types.

We had a regular meeting every morning before clocking off, when the foremen and manager summed up the night's work and any issues that had come up. They spoke for three minutes, if that. There was also a brief huddle before the shift started, for setting priorities or discussing any matters that needed attention. It was tedious, but over quickly. I normally didn't listen. After all, talk does not a revolution make.

When I completed my trial, an assistant foreman, a short guy, pulled me aside for a chat. Our team had one main and three assistant foremen then, and above all of them a manager in charge of admin. This guy told me that although the probationary period wasn't paid, he would make it up by giving me three extra days of vacation. This was back when we didn't need to punch in. I was pleased to hear this, of course. But it wasn't even a month before the same guy had a dispute with the other foremen and quit. No one mentioned those paid days off ever again.

D Company had its core business in logistics, but in 2013 it had also rolled out an express delivery service that hadn't developed like hoped, and when I joined in 2017 it only had a negligible share of the market. Unfortunately, this did not translate to an easier time for those of us who handled its parcels. Staffing had a direct correlation with workload, and capitalists aren't known for sympathizing with slackers.

In my first months there, I rotated between unpacking and packing. There were four roles in our team: The unpackers worked in sync with labeling, and shelving worked alongside packing. The unpackers emptied the giant sacks of parcels onto the sorting floor and the labelers scanned the barcodes on the order form, writing the destination postal code for each parcel on its front in pen. Then the marked parcels were passed down the line into the packing area, where the shelvers put them into the various shelves based on destination. The packers would then bag each shelf of parcels individually and carry the labeled bags onto the forklift to be taken to the loading bay. In terms of intensity, labeling was the lightest work and was often done by women.

At the end of the shift, everyone went to eat breakfast. To us, this was really our dinner, the second of the two meals we had each day. Then we returned to our dorms to wash ourselves and our clothes. The uniform proved impossible to ever get fully clean. We lifted and moved goods for hours on end—grease and oil stains were inevitable. Plus, it was easy to convince ourselves when we were already tired that we didn't need to make sure our clothes were pristine. They were only going to get dirty again the next day. With good-quality stain remover the price it was, if we did attempt to clean them, we settled for a bar of soap. But this wouldn't get rid of the strong odor of sweat that lingered even after air-drying. Doing this type of work though, people naturally stopped caring.

Anyway, it was sleep that caused the most problems—not everyone adapted well to the upside-down schedule. My first few months there, I would be too exhausted to function by four or five o'clock every morning. If I only lay down, I would nod off in seconds; and if lying down wasn't possible, then I might still drop off at any moment. Sometimes, I would black out as if I was about to lose consciousness before jolting awake again, instantly, and grabbing at whatever was nearby to hold me upright. I was like the walking dead—a thousand-yard stare and a foggy mind, and no idea what I had been doing only a second earlier. I mixed up two labels when I was in this state: stuck a Beijing label on a package meant for Chongqing, and the Chongqing label on the Beijing package. Luckily, the mistake was spotted, and the parcels were brought back before they had been loaded onto the trucks. I'm not exaggerating when I say that every shift, when the lack of sleep had me up against a wall, I used to swear to myself that I was going to hit the hay immediately after work, regardless of what else needed my attention. Except that by the time I got off in the morning, the fatigue had always passed, and I suddenly had my energy back. It always came with a strange sense of restlessness as well, like I had labored for so long in a way my body didn't like that it now craved an activity it enjoyed; I had to shake off the lethargy and replenish my being and my strength. A lot of colleagues went to karaoke after their shift for this very reason, and they stayed there until it started to get dark again, squeezing in only an hour or two of sleep before work. But that was wild to me; I didn't want to lose my life to work. My approach was to try to be kind with myself. Like I would eat an extra-good breakfast or go for a stroll around the supermarket in town. It was only a small supermarket, with a limited selection, but I found that walking up and down the aisles relieved stress, even if all I bought in the end was one or two things.

The trouble was that I still didn't feel like sleeping afterward. And I couldn't, anyway, even if I tried. By the afternoon, I would start worrying about getting no rest once again. The room I stayed in when I first started was hot and stuffy. In summer, the temperature inside could get up to ninety degrees. The walls were scalding hot from the sun, and my fan didn't make a dent. I was renting a room without AC, to save money, even though an upgrade only cost fifty yuan more. It must have been early August when I decided I couldn't take it any longer. I felt like I was cooking to death. I contacted the landlady to ask if I could change rooms. But in what world would there be a room with air conditioning going free in summer? The landlady, though, kept up the pretense that there would be one available soon. She strung me out like this for two months, past the mid-Autumn festival, then finally got in touch with an offer. The weather was cooler by then, but it was still uncomfortable; October in Guangdong can mean temperatures in the eighties. I jumped at the chance, only to use the AC a total of three or four times, maximum, before the heat started to ease off.

Noise was another factor in my struggle to get to sleep. The block where my room was didn't have a call system at the main door. Any visitors therefore had two choices: either call the person they were coming to see on their cell, so they would come down and open the door, or stand outside and shout up. The hollering never failed to make me want to run downstairs and throttle whoever just woke me.

My room had thin walls, too, and I overheard the neighbors arguing once. The husband was shouting at the wife. There was a lot of name-calling and yelling, but the wife didn't say a word the whole time. Maybe she was the one in the wrong. The husband shouted that when he came back from such a hard shift, all he wanted was to get a good sleep, but even that he couldn't do . . . I guess something the wife had done had upset him. Then he started to cry—a grown man crying and yelling. I'm not immune to gossip, so I tried to listen for any hint as to what the wife had done. But I could only understand very little of what he said. We were people from all over the country in that place, and we each had our own accents, some of them foreign to me.

For all that though, I still had trouble sleeping even when it was quiet out and a more bearable temperature. I'd tried everything that might help. Sleeping pills I couldn't find, but I had heard that dark chocolate worked almost the same, so I dosed it like it was medicine—a square before bed every night—but this did nothing, of course. I also went for melatonin, with absolutely no effect. In the end I had to resort to the tried-and-true method of drinking. The supermarket sold a range of *erguotou* sorghum liquor in four-liter bottles. The Red Star stuff was too expensive, so I just bought the knockoff brands.

Most of them were produced in Sichuan (rather than Beijing), and they went down nowhere near as cleanly as the kind I was used to. They were almost pungent. But they were cheap, and that's what counted. With my self-imposed budget, I could also stretch to something of slightly better quality on occasion. Five hundred milliliters of Old Village, at eighteen yuan a bottle, was the best I could find at that price.

While I drank, I liked to read, though I never had any memory of what I'd read afterward. Sometimes it took as much as four ounces of spirits before I felt ready to lie down. The goal was to be asleep before 2 P.M., so I could be up by half past six; maybe when I managed that, I would rejoice.

On the awful days when I was still awake past four, my anxiety went through the roof. Before I started at D Company, I used to sleep seven hours a day; but working nights, I averaged four.

The big problem with the drinking was that I would still be tipsy when I woke up. Fortunately, I walked to work. I felt every dip and bump underfoot, as I went, though I couldn't say if it was me that was swaying or the world. When I drank less, it was like I hadn't had any rest at all. I passed by a row of houses on my way in every day. I could smell the cooking going on inside, see the people collapsed on their couches, tired and content after a day's work. That, to me, was what true happiness looked like. Meanwhile I was already more exhausted than those people, and I hadn't even reached the warehouse. I cursed myself in those moments: My damned body cursed my willpower, and my damned willpower cursed it back. I swore I would go right to sleep when I clocked off in the morning. But then the morning came around, and everything went the same as the day before. I was trapped in a loop.

I should say something about where I was staying at the time. It was in a village called Luoheng that was separated from the logistics park by a small stream. The logistics park was a development zone that had no perimeter fence or security gate. Vehicles and people could come and go as they pleased. But Luoheng was closed off by the stream on one side and a gate, which was shut at ten every evening, on the other. This seemed strange to me, at first. Why would a village need to be isolated like that? I hadn't come across it before. Later, I learned that Luoheng's main industry was ornamental plants, everything from exquisite bonsai to tall, lush trees for lining avenues. Some of the plants must have been valuable, so the locals wanted to protect them against theft. Even just for my walk to and from work, I had to hop a barbed wire fence. One day, when it was raining and I had an umbrella with me, I slipped when I was climbing over and slapped my right hand down on a spike. I still have the scar today.

The villagers in Luoheng all shared a surname, Yun. Based on the couplets pasted up outside their ancestral halls, I understood that their families had moved there from Longzhong when China still had dynasties. The village was originally called Luokeng—this I discovered when I came across the discarded plaque of an old house. Changing the village's name from one that included the word for "pit" to one that suggested "luck" or "prosperity" felt dishonest somehow. But I can appreciate the locals thinking that calling their hometown a pit might hurt trade. Imagine you're a small business owner in the Pearl River Delta wanting to spruce up your office with some lucky bamboo; plants from Luoheng Village are going to be much more appealing than those from Luokeng.

The thing was, living in Luoheng was inconvenient. There wasn't a supermarket there, or a hairdresser, or restaurant, just two convenience stores that had a small range of products. Most of my colleagues stayed in Shizhou, a bigger town nearby. It took half an hour to walk there, a trip I made every second or third day to do the groceries. Shizhou had a vegetable market, a small park, a basketball court, a midsize supermarket, and several stores. There were also a lot of small eateries and rooms for rent, and some street food stalls that opened in the evening for barbecue and mini hotpot. But I liked the quiet, so Luoheng still suited me better. Plus, rent was slightly cheaper. My room, for example, was four hundred yuan for the month, but the same room would have cost five hundred in Shizhou.

None of us really shopped online while living in Luoheng, even though you could buy anything you could think of on the internet, and for less expensive than otherwise. Delivery drivers just refused to come to our doors, or even enter the village. They stopped at the gate and rang our cells, so we'd go out and meet them. It took ten minutes to walk from my building to the gate, and there was no way to tell what time a courier might show up. Daytime rest being so precious and fragile, I preferred not to risk a phone call, in case sleep eluded me afterward. So, I made do with what I could find in Shizhou, instead. Luckily, this often meant getting a lot for my money, like the Triangle brand kettle I bought for only twenty-nine yuan and left behind when I moved. Anything pricier wouldn't find a buyer in Shizhou.

The D Company warehouse epitomized the old saying about a sturdy barracks through which soldiers readily flow. Basically, people tended not to stick around for very long, so the company was always hiring. When I had just joined, it was offering a three-hundred-yuan commission if you could refer someone. This later became five hundred—then eight hundred—and jumped to one thousand yuan in the runup to the Singles' Day sales on November 11. I earned five hundred by referring a friend to the sales office for a courier job. But I didn't take a single *fen*; I gave it all to him. Only, he hadn't been working for two months when he quit, saying he was overtired.

Stuck up in the sorting-floor restrooms, next to the hot water machines, and over the sinks were color HR posters that shared employees' stories about their time at work. I still remember a few of them now. One was from someone who had been on the sorting floor for several years before leaving to start his own business. Let's call him Wang because I've obviously forgotten his name. He then lost all his money and came back. Now he was saying that it was good to work with your hands, and that the company had looked after him . . . The quote ran next to a photo portrait. He looked to be doing okay in the picture, flashing a happy and contented smile at the camera. There were lots of others with similar experiences to Wang who were displayed for us to look at while we urinated, washed our hands, or filled our bottles.

As well as concocting posters, HR personnel got out on the front line themselves, setting up stalls on street corners in Shizhou, pinning up Now Hiring flyers and posting ads on apps. They were tireless, trying every avenue under the sun. They didn't much care who answered their call: Applicants were sent straight to the sorting floor for a trial. HR had its own KPI targets to meet, after all. This probably accounted for the fair number of hopefuls on trial who clearly weren't a good fit.

One girl who arrived one evening, with spindly limbs and a small frame, did not look at all cut out for manual labor. But she was still assigned to the sorting floor, and it wasn't like we could send her back to HR or pass her off onto another team.

We just had to let her try. The foreman, though, was reluctant to hire anyone who might be slow, since they threatened the productivity of the whole team. Plus, they usually left after only a month or two when the work proved too tough. It was pointless bringing her in. During her trial, the team leader specifically warned us not to help her.

Like I mentioned previously, the trial was the hardest toil anyone would ever do there, and that was only the start of a long week or two for people unaccustomed to heavy lifting. Those in bad shape could forget about acclimatizing, entirely. The frailer a person, the less we were supposed to support them—we didn't want to give anyone the false belief that they could manage. So, we had to put her through the wringer, and if she still stayed, then so be it. The other side of the coin was that we were encouraged to help those who looked strong as much as we wanted.

During my own trial, I struggled to crack the technique for emptying the large polypropylene bags of parcels quickly. I could flip them okay, but I was using my index fingers like hooks to yank and shake the material from over the parcels, instead of simply pinching the bag's tail between forefinger and thumb, and pulling. It felt fine at first doing it my way, there was no pain, but after three nights of handling the bags like this, the nails on both my index fingers were bent backward. They turned black some days later and eventually fell off. It was almost three months before they grew back.

All of this said, we did have some people with disabilities working with us. Government policy required that every company hired a proportional number. D Company had apparently failed to meet the quota in the past and been fined a large sum. They were good workers, though. In a few roles, there was no telling the difference between them and the rest of us. Some disabilities just hindered people from switching to other posts. Anyone with a limp, for example, couldn't do unpacking or packing, because of all the walking back and forth those jobs required—I wore through a pair of brand-new Decathlon sneakers in four months. This inevitably complicated things for the foreman when it came to drawing up the schedule, so he didn't like them on the team, and he sometimes made this known.

In any team, there is always someone who is excluded, and ours was no exception. For us, it was a nineteen-year-old woman straight out of school. She was younger than most of us, slight of build, and neither quick nor strong. She might even have been a little slow. She often held back the line, forcing others to help her and sometimes to pause the conveyor belt. She was also quite odd, and got along with nobody particularly well. Pretty much everyone disliked her, actually: They gave her ugly nicknames, made fun of her to her face, and criticized her. If that had been me, I would have immediately dropped out. But she was clearly the more resilient of the two of us, or the more numb, and cared less about what people thought. Either way, she stayed on for a long time, way longer than I had expected. I was as friendly with her as I could be, given her situation. The one time she was pushed to crying in anger, she ran off in the middle of the shift, saying she wasn't doing it anymore. The foreman sighed with relief. He had been trying to swap out all the low-efficiency workers, but this young woman had been insistent that she wanted to persevere. The foreman could do nothing. Two days later, she told him that she wanted to come back and he, of course, refused. Her boyfriend, who also worked on the sorting floor in loading, brought her over to ask nicely, and the three of them debated it for a long time: All of us who worked at the company saw each other whether we wanted to or not, and we were all workers; what was the good in being so hard on one another? The foreman eventually gave in, and the woman returned to our ranks, and to the constant torment.

Some days after I joined, I was followed by another newcomer. On his first day the foreman made me show him the canteen, and the guy clung to me every day after that. He wanted to arrange meeting somewhere on the way to work, so we could walk in together. He even suggested that we take the same days off and make plans. Luckily, the manager didn't allow it. Everyone else assumed that we knew each other from before. He made me uncomfortable, to be honest, but I felt awkward saying no. He was just being friendly. But he did have a weakness—he loved to brag. He was always going on about how impressive he was, the things he knew how to do, and all the people he had set straight in his life. He could take on six people at once, that kind of thing. I just listened and nodded. I didn't dare to tell him that I didn't believe him. I used to wonder how little self-esteem he must have, how hollow he felt, to need to blow his own horn like that all the time. Looking back, I understand him a little better. He and I had accepted offers of work somewhere neither of us knew anyone, at about the same time. We shared many of the same standpoints, concerns, and interests. We would both benefit from being allies. Going it alone in a new environment is risky business. If you're unlucky, you could end up ostracized like that young woman. He realized all this the very first time we met, whereas I was oblivious. It's only now that I see what he was trying to do.

There was also a pregnant woman who joined our team. She was referred by her boyfriend who was already a colleague. There had been an HR rule previously that partners couldn't work together, but the boyfriend must have hidden their relationship at the outset. Once it was a done thing, the foreman could only let her stay. She wasn't showing when she first arrived. She was in her early twenties, and healthy, and she had no problem completing the tasks. But her bump slowly grew, and it became difficult to watch her work. We went all through the night, after all. One colleague, shaking their head, called it one of "mankind's tragedies" that she even had to be there.

The young woman's boyfriend liked to gamble. Actually, he played the Mark Six lottery on an app, but it was essentially the same thing. Days after our salaries came in, he had already blown his whole paycheck, so he would use his girlfriend's for food and rent. He even made her ask to borrow money from us, because he was too embarrassed to keep asking himself. Eventually, they started to fight. Mostly it was she who was taking issue with him. He had a good temper, to be fair—he never lost his cool—but what use is a good temper? It's like putting a lid on a pot without a bottom. In the end she ran off, in the middle of a shift, crying. Probably the combination of tiredness and anger had become too much. She quit the next day, and I never saw her again, whereas the guy was still there when I left. He had found a new girlfriend not long after the breakup, a married woman who had moved away from home to find work. You could see the look of shame on his face any time someone mentioned his pregnant ex. He told us he sent her child support, but I have no idea if this was true. He did give up gambling, though. Maybe he just couldn't sponge any more money, or maybe the app had been blocked.

We had witnessed all of this unfold, quiet onlookers, none of us stepping in to teach him a lesson or reaching out to help the pregnant woman. At most there were some words of comfort offered to her. We each had our own pressures to deal with in the end, our own issues at home. No one had anything left over to give. A work environment like that squeezes all life from a person. You wind up emotionally overdrawn, and numb and indifferent, without even noticing.

This job could really ruin a person's temper. With all those long nights, and the overworking, it was noticeably harder to control one's emotions.

I had arguments with two different people in my team, fierce fights both times. One of them slacked too much when partnered with me on the job. He also had a bad attitude and a sharp tongue. He thought that taking advantage of people was the normal thing to do.

The other guy was much worse. He pushed all the hardest tasks onto me and kept all the easiest stuff for himself. He never even bothered to hide that this was what he was doing. We very nearly came to blows.

I had this urge to fight at the time that wouldn't go away, it didn't matter with who, and he was a particularly good candidate. But a physical altercation would lead to dismissal—this included people who met up outside work to settle disputes, if the company found out. So, I was glad I didn't go through with it.

Generally, everyone in the team was pretty tolerant of people loafing around, since we all agreed that our workload and income would never be fair. As long as slackers weren't a burden, everyone turned a blind eye. And in a way, the biggest offenders were the easiest to get along with. Probably because they had a guilty conscience.

While I'm on the topic, this was how our salary was calculated: There were some fifty of us in our team. We were ranked either A, B, or C according to our performance each month. The top ten performers were given an A grade, while anyone who committed a serious mistake, like losing a parcel, sorting incorrectly, skipping work, or disobeying instructions, received a C; the rest got a B. Remuneration for A grades was just over 5,000 yuan; for Bs it was about 4,700; and for Cs it was around 4,300. These base amounts would fluctuate in line with the total number of parcels processed every month. Since C was the penalty grade, we could avoid it as long as we didn't make any mistakes. So essentially, everyone was either an A or a B.

Some people cared more than others about which one they ended up getting, like the second person I argued with. If ever he wasn't ranked A, he demanded an explanation from the foreman and tried to pressure the company into upgrading him. Most people, though, accepted their fate without question. Even if they complained occasionally, they never tried to secure anything more than they were given. These folks either didn't want the extra toil, or they were confident that since it was so hard to stand out, they were better off doing a little less. It was easier this way to avoid slipups that might land them a C. The first bozo I argued with was in this category.

Our performance in a month, and so the grade we were given, was supposed to be based on the number of parcels we processed. But a fair comparison of output was impossible when our roles and tasks were different. So, the parcel count oftentimes just felt like something the foreman dangled in front of our faces to encourage us, or something he used to fob us off. His main considerations, when he doled out our grades, were keeping everyone happy and charging up the better workers who put in the most effort, which meant we all got our turn being an A.

I was someone who always gave my work my all and tried my best to get along with others. I had my disagreements with those slackers, sure, but everyone else had been relieved to see them called out. I'd go so far as to say that I was the team's friendliest and most amenable member. I said thank you more often than the rest of the team combined. For this reason, and thanks to my performance, I ranked A five times in the ten months I was at D Company, which altogether made for a good salary. To me, this said the foreman recognized the effort I was putting in. Those five As were the most he could have possibly given me without ruffling the feathers of more senior employees: It would not have been wise of him to give me an A in either of my first two months or the month that I quit. The A grade was a precious, limited resource; almost everyone had their eyes set on it.

Newcomers generally weren't awarded As, because the foreman couldn't risk wasting one on someone who was only going to quit the next week. He had to make every A count.

There was also an employee of the month award, which everybody in the team voted for anonymously. I won first place twice in my first three months, and second place another month. The manager changed the voting method soon after, to stop a few people from dominating. My prizes were some household products and a blow-dryer, which I gave to a colleague with longer hair who had more use for it.

The logistics park where D Company was located also contained a few outsourcing companies, which we would rely on for extra hands to deal with the increased orders during the peak season or a big promotional push from an e-commerce platform. The temp workers themselves tended to go slower than the rest of us, since they were never in any role long enough to refine their skills. They were also paid by the day. There was no letter ranking for them, they only had to do a passable job to receive their paycheck. No need to try hard. We had a love-hate relationship with these workers: We looked forward to their help because they alleviated some of the pressure on us, but to watch how they worked was infuriating.

Worse was, they could do no wrong: Their company operated in a seller's market. If they gave D Company a low rating, then their employer could refuse to work together in the future, and D Company would have to shell out more to secure their services for the next peak season.

We would jokingly rib each other, when someone was slacking, "You're so lazy, why don't you go work with the temps?" But there were people who really left to join the outsourcing company. The benefit of that was the freedom. You could choose the number of days you wanted to do in a month.

Still, D Company was publicly listed, and was the pride of the goods logistics business, which meant it was regulated and law-abiding. It provided full insurance coverage to its employees, for one, and it never fell behind on wages. We all had to weigh up the pros and cons for ourselves.

For example, nobody would call working in logistics a risky profession, but there was still the occasional death on the sorting floor. With several hundred people regularly employed at any one time, and the constant flow and turnover of personnel, a conservative estimate of how many people worked there in the space of a year was several thousand. Some of those people inevitably had underlying conditions that might be set off through overwork and kill them quite suddenly. The year I was there, a loader died. He had been working like crazy to load two trucks in a single night. He went home to lie down and never got up again.

In 2018, before the Spring Festival, the stock management department made a WeChat group and invited four or five hundred of us to join. The annual tradition was that the foremen and team managers would take turns posting "red envelopes" on the chat for everyone to try to claim. So, I spent New Year's Eve, the thirtieth of the last lunar month, in bed cashing red envelopes and taking in the holiday atmosphere. I had never been part of a group chat with so many people before. Everyone was chatting and sharing pictures of their families, wishing each other a good year ahead, and bickering and bantering. There were all the New Year's emojis and GIFs flying back and forth. The conversation kept jumping ahead by a dozen screens' worth of chatter in one go, causing my phone to freeze. There was more action happening on my screen than on the televised New Year's Eve gala. It had been such a long time since my Spring Festival had felt so warm and excitement filled. They had been so dull in past years.

My phone must have been too crappy, or the internet too slow, because there were lots of red envelopes I missed even if I clicked on them. In the end I only collected fifteen or so yuan which I sent right back into the group. Happiness is something that money can't buy.

I forget if it was before or after the festival, but our team manager took some of us out one night for hot pot. This was a new manager who started when the previous one was transferred to another province. This replacement had worked his way up from the bottom of another department and immediately set to winning over the main players in our team, so he could have everyone's support. As well as some foremen and one assistant, he invited four regular team members, one of which was me. His meaning was clear: He saw me as a backup foreman.

When I eventually resigned, I heard that D Company was planning to build a new transfer center in Dongping, in the Baiyun district of Guangzhou. This manager had intended to recommend me for a position there. Our logistics park was in C Village in Shunde, and though it was technically part of Foshan, it took longer to reach the city center than it did Guangzhou South Station, in the next prefecture over, which was barely half an hour away by bike.

But if I still worked there today, I would be a reserve manager, at best, and probably pulling my hair out and screaming at anyone and everyone around me. I heard that doing night shifts for prolonged periods increases the risk of developing Alzheimer's too. I wasn't young anymore, even then, and that possibility was no longer so distant a future that I could afford not to think about it. I could already feel my mind slowing down, my reactions becoming duller, my memory fading. I started to eat nuts to fight degeneration, regardless of whether they actually helped or not. Because of the price, I mostly bought walnuts, peanuts, and roasted seeds.

There used to be dozens of different kinds of peanuts and seeds for sale in Shizhou, all for under ten yuan for a five-hundred-gram bag, and I must have tried almost every one of them. There were also walnuts, with a softer shell, for the same price. They weren't like the hard ones I used to eat as a kid, so hard they could bend the hinges on a door; and they were different from the ones available online from Xinjiang, with paper-thin skin that would break at a touch. They were somewhere in the middle. I threw them at the ground to crack the shell, then picked out the kernel. But I do know that walnuts can't prevent Alzheimer's.

I left D Company, and Guangdong Province, in March 2018 and moved to Beijing. Not for work, but for a woman. I still thank myself every day that I made this leap of faith.

My relationship with my girlfriend Juneau is as strong as ever now. We got to know each other through a writing forum, from about 2011 onward. We never communicated beyond that website for years, then one day in 2017, we started to talk on WeChat, for a reason I can't remember. She had found herself at a low point in her life, and I was not doing so well myself. We understood each other in that regard, how to value and support one another, the way people let down by life often do. For the Spring Festival in 2018, I used the few days of holiday to go to Beijing, to meet her in person.

When I returned to Shunde after that short trip, I immediately handed in my one month's notice. The company let me go early, after two weeks, when it became apparent they would have no trouble finding a replacement in the post-holiday rush for jobs. Plus, it was slack season.

I hadn't really thought about what I was going to do for a living once I got to Beijing. I was confident I'd find something; I had a low bar and no qualms about hard work. Juneau didn't care how much money I earned either. She still doesn't. She has never made any demands of me financially. We share a lot of the same views when it comes to life and writing, it's the main reason I feel so sure about the future. We might not have a *fen* between us, but as long as we care for each other, and face it together, she won't give up on me, nor I on her.

I joined S Company soon after arriving in the capital and became a courier, no longer having to work nights. Doing deliveries is hard work, but there's no need to stay up late to do it, and the income was higher. I should have become a courier all along. I have trouble socializing, and I thought back then that delivering parcels would be difficult for me because of how much customer interaction it would require daily. But I soon realized that I was more than up to the task.

As I write, I've been in Beijing for three years. Three years passed in the blink of an eye. I've left S Company now, and soon I'll leave Beijing. Thinking back on who I was at D Company, I've changed a lot already, but some things have stayed the same. For instance, I don't have an urge to argue anymore, and especially not to fight; but I do still eat walnuts, peanuts, and seeds whenever I can.

2

I Deliver Parcels in Beijing

Interview

I went for the interview at S Company on my third day in Beijing. I had spent the two days before settling in and, straight out of bed on the morning of the third, uploaded my résumé to the job-search site 58.com. It was March 20. I received the phone call before I had even eaten lunch.

The woman on the other end made it clear immediately that she wasn't from the employing company but from a headhunting service under 58.com's banner—a subsidiary. At first, I assumed she was trying to sell me something, but she assured me that her responsibility was to help to connect people seeking jobs with companies offering them. She had looked over my résumé and believed that I was a suitable candidate to refer for an opening at S Company, a parcel service. If I had time in the afternoon, she continued, would I be available for an interview in Yizhuang? She would text me the address.

Yes, I answered, without a second thought.

Putting lots of hours into finding the best job didn't seem worthwhile, as far as I was concerned. My qualifications would never secure anything with good pay, and S Company was a far better prospect than the worst-case scenario I'd been imagining.

I was about to set off for Yizhuang when another call came. A different woman asked me if I had any interest in trialing for a position at D Company.

I told her that I had officially left D Company not a week earlier, and the manager had said at the time that it normally took former employees a minimum of three months before they could find new employment. Did moving cities cancel this out, I wondered aloud.

She didn't answer. I had included my employment history on the résumé I posted online, along with my D Company leaving date, so she can't have read it very carefully. After some faltering, she said she would look into this for me and follow up later. Unsurprisingly, she didn't contact me again.

My interview would turn out to be the only time I ever went to Yizhuang. The location was an industrial park open to the public, surrounded by an enormous factory area. The S Company building stood on the roadside looking a little worn down. It was very obviously a site where manual labor took place. But oddly, there was nobody around.

I remember there being a dozen of us applicants standing in a room listening to a manager speak. But whether there were any chairs in there or we just felt too awkward to sit down, I'm not sure. Anyway, the manager also remained standing. I never quite figured out whom or what he managed, but he was the only person we interacted with the whole time. He took a casual tone with us. He too had been a courier once, he said, had worked his way up from there, and now he was in HR. The point he probably wanted to put across was that we started in the same place, him and us, workers all of us, and we too could get to where he was one day.

So, we gathered around him in a circle and listened attentively. He raised his voice to make sure everybody would hear, like he was a tour guide announcing the local sights to a group of paying customers. His job wasn't all that different from a tour guide's, come to think of it. There was a lot of talk online, he explained, about couriers having long earned more than ten thousand yuan a month, and people had inevitably begun to assume that delivering parcels meant a high income—this was certainly true for some couriers, but they were in the minority. New hires who hadn't yet built up a network of clients wouldn't be able to make so much for quite a while. But he was quick to add that the company guaranteed a minimum of five thousand yuan for the first month.

He went on to say that it was demanding work, with difficult customers and long hours spent outside regardless of the weather. That people normally think it's a walk in the park, until they try it and find it's too tough, even for them... Clearly, he was less concerned that we were underqualified or that we looked down on the job, and more that if we were going to quit after a couple of days anyway, we were better off doing it then and there. That's how it sounded to me. But I never had any illusions about five-figure pay or an easy time, and neither did the others, I assume, since nobody walked out disappointed or asked a question.

Satisfied that we were all tempering our expectations, the manager produced a stack of forms for us to fill in. After we'd done this, he let us choose which nearby depot we wanted to report to. He did so by reading out the names of all the ones in the area with vacancies, and we raised our hands to register. The first name he read was for a place I'd never heard of, though this was no surprise since I didn't know 99 percent of Beijing. A part of me worried that he might reach the last site on the list without me having recognized a single name—what would I do then? But luckily the very next place he pronounced was Liyuan—right where I was staying. Beijing being as big as it is, and with so many districts and neighborhoods, I couldn't believe he would say my new home second. This was fate giving me a shove in the back, so up my hand went.

Once I had the depot address and the phone number of the person in charge, I confirmed on Gaode Maps that it was only a twenty-minute walk between there and my place. Seeing that it was still early, I decided there was no point in delaying another day. I called L, the depot director, to confirm I would be there soon to sign in, but the Beijing traffic decided to teach me a lesson. I hit the evening rush heading back from Yizhuang, and after being stuck for two hours I had to phone the director again to say I wouldn't make it in until the next morning.

Beijing in March could still be bitingly cold. The temperature sat around a dozen degrees lower than the southern city I'd left behind. I traveled the following morning to a neighborhood complex along Yunjing South Avenue where the Yunjing depot was located. Director L's office was on the second floor. Before I entered, I saw there were also depots for JD.com and D Company next door. These gated residential complexes were popular among businesses needing office or storage space. It must have been all the comings and goings of the various companies' trucks that got the sidewalk so cracked and potholed.

Director L oversaw four of the company depots in the area, including the one in Yunjing. In that first meeting, I discovered there were still questions I had to answer for what must have been the official interview to be complete.

L wore thin-framed glasses and looked to be around forty years old. He smiled politely when he spoke. He can't have been very busy that day, because he seemed in no rush to get to the point. The issue was, I hadn't mentally prepared myself for one-on-one conversation, so he did most of the talking, and I just answered his questions.

I told him where I was from, how long I had been in Beijing—just four days, I said—and he asked me why I wanted to be a courier. In fact, I wasn't convinced that I did want to be a courier. If there had been a better option, I would have gone for that, instead. This wasn't the answer he wanted to hear though, clearly, and I didn't dare risk it. But I still made a mistake. I should have led with how I'd always been impressed by S Company—joining a company you like is a perfectly reasonable thing to do, and this would have been a fine answer. But my nerves got the better of me and I said it was because I was staying nearby and I didn't want to travel far to work. Now this was true, of course, but it wasn't the whole truth—of the jobs available to me, being a courier also offered the best pay. But it came out like I didn't care, like I was only there for an easy time, and hadn't given much thought to the decision.

Sure enough, L took umbrage. How long was I planning to stay in Beijing, he probed, the insinuation clear. Why had I come here in the first place? Once I gave my responses, he moved on to my home situation and my parents' ages and if I had any children. I knew what he was worried about, so I made sure to be extra careful in my further answers. I thought he'd be happy with what I said, but he just insisted that this gig wasn't as good as I was imagining.

I wasn't imagining it to be good at all, I admitted.

He then explained that delivering parcels is a lot of hard work.

I wasn't afraid of hard work, I told him. My last job had been much tougher than delivering parcels.

Talk like this made me feel awkward. I knew what he was so concerned about: that I would do the job for a few days, then vanish. Enough people did, apparently, and it must have given him a headache. From our conversation up to this point, he had learned that I didn't have children, and that my parents had medical insurance and pensions and had no need for my support. I had very few obligations. This put him on guard. It surprised me that he was so sensitive to this sort of thing. He was clearly worried that if anything infelicitous happened while I was at work, I could simply quit, instead of bearing the brunt, and not worry about the effect on others. On top of this, he probably thought that I sounded too refined when I spoke, compared with other new recruits. He might have been cultured himself, but I later got the sense that he preferred his delivery drivers to be coarse, since they were less likely to have a surfeit of confidence. Later on, I would see for myself how self-esteem could be a hindrance to work.

Looking back today, I can understand his attitude and why he treated me the way he did: If I had been in his shoes, I would have done the same if it meant doing a good job. He tried dissuading me, but gently, since like me he wasn't the type to be blunt. And, critically, he would have needed a very good reason for turning me away after I had already traveled to Yizhuang and been assigned to him. But he took me on, in the end, even if he seemed reluctant, and put me down for a trial the next day at the nearby Linhe depot.

Trial and Onboarding

S Company's Linhe depot was once genuinely by the riverside, as the Chinese name suggested, but when the site was closed after failing a fire safety inspection, it was moved to the back yard of an office building kitty-corner to Liyuan metro station. Only the name remained. I learned this from Gao. He was the courier who took me out for my trial shifts—he was my *shifu*—even though he was much younger. He was born in the northeast in 1995.

Gao covered part of the area where Liyuan Middle Street and Yuqiao East Road met. He was responsible for the Xingfu

Artspace, Wellspring Gardens, and Yuqiao East neighborhood complexes. The three neighborhoods stood right up against each other, separated only by metal fences.

The first time I rode on the back of Gao's electric trike, he told me that he actually had two trikes for making deliveries. One of them was having issues and was sitting at home, so he had taken one of the depot's. "So-and-so has been working here for almost ten years, and he still drives that same piece of junk he did when he started. And I have two trikes of my own," he boasted, proudly.

It seemed like a strange way of looking at the situation to me, treating the vehicles as if they were his personal property. I've forgotten the name of the colleague in question now because I ended up rarely working with him, and I didn't try to confirm if he had really worked there for ten years, either. But his trike definitely stood out as different. It was an older model. I didn't know at the time that Gao was in an ongoing dispute with the depot staff for having made off with the extra trike. He and his girlfriend drove it to do their groceries during his breaks, he told me with just as much pride. He was clearly delighted with the "perk" of using a company vehicle for personal errands.

The S Company trial was unpaid and lasted three days, but there was no requirement during it to do any work. The idea was simply to shadow *shifu*. Though in reality, of course, I had to help—who would be brazen enough to stand back and watch, without lifting a finger? So, Gao and I worked together. He parked outside an apartment block, and we took a staircase each. Gao knew the neighborhoods well and filled me in on which places the residents would be home and which they wouldn't; and if nobody was going to be in, where I should leave the parcel: in the entranceway, on the shoe rack, or inside the box for the electric meter . . . The job seemed easy at this point. A good memory and time were all that were needed to learn an area and find your flow.

On my third afternoon of the trial, I carved out some hours to go for a checkup at the hospital affiliated with the China Construction Second Engineering Bureau, next to the depot. I was told I could collect my results in three days. If I had known I would have to wait, I'd have done the checkup before starting the trial. Instead, I lost out on a day's work.

Fortunately, Gao got in touch the next morning to ask for help with an overly large assignment he would struggle to finish on his own. I had nothing else going on, and it was a good opportunity to familiarize myself with the neighborhoods, so I went along. When we were done, he took me to a nearby market, where we had lunch at Chengdu Staples. His way of saying thank you. I had worked for free, so I didn't argue.

There were six members in Gao's team altogether. The other drivers covered Binjiang Royal View, Jingyi Clearsky

Gardens, and Meiran Baidu City. After the morning scramble, with fewer parcels to deliver in the afternoons and time not as tight, the team would meet by the gate for Binjiang Royal View and shoot the breeze while they waited for the next drop.

That afternoon there was another new recruit there, a young guy assigned to the south side of the neighborhood, who told me, "If you slip the nurses an extra fifty yuan, you don't have to wait for three days for the medical report. It's ready the next day."

"The nurse didn't say anything when I asked if they could do it quicker," I said.

"They drag it out on purpose, to make more money. Asking is no good, you have to just pay. She won't say anything, otherwise. It's against the rules." This was his experience, anyway. It was up to me if I believed him or not, but he gained nothing from lying to me. Still, I trusted the nurse I had spoken to, she looked like she took her responsibilities very seriously. At the end of the shift, Gao arranged for me to come back and help out the next day as well. I was happy to.

After finishing our deliveries the following morning, I went to the hospital and collected my medical report, which I then submitted to the depot manager. This was Z. I quickly got the impression that Z wasn't the friendliest person, or much of a talker. Besides ignoring most of the questions I asked him, he barely looked at me. I felt like a junior school student talking to a teacher. Obviously, I had done nothing wrong, but I couldn't shake the feeling he was being condescending. I had completed two days of interviews, then three days' probation, so by the time the physical report was ready another three days later, it was already March 27.

Manager Z made me sit off to the side while he used the computer on his desk, though I couldn't say if it was for anything to do with me. After a bit of a wait, he informed me that there were no more vacancies for March. The soonest I could start was April 2.

Now is when you decide to tell me there are no openings, I remember thinking. Regardless of whether this made sense or not, it showed a fundamental lack of respect. If there were no jobs going, then why advertise for hire? There wasn't even a hint of an apology in his voice either. His expression just said: Do you want to do this or not?

First thing the next day Gao called again, asking for a favor. The depot was pushing him to return the trike he had commandeered, and he needed a hand with the older one, which he still had to take to be repaired. From how frustrated he was when I found him, I assumed he'd had another argument with the depot staff. I got the sense he belonged to the less disciplined and more troublemaking contingent of the workers in our area.

We towed the broken trike with the working one to Chunjia Alley Park neighborhood off Linhe Inner Road, where there was a mini repair shop with a door no bigger than a yard wide. Gao left me behind to wait while he went to do his rounds. I sat there twiddling my thumbs, looking around at the inside of the shop. I still remember it now: the pitted cement of the floor and its oily black sheen. The various vehicle parts piled in a muddle up against the walls (though the owner might well have seen some order there).

There were two customers who came by for batteries: an older woman who collected the one she had reserved and handed over six or seven hundred yuan, which was less than I'd expected, and a middle-aged man who eventually left without buying. I remember trivial details like those, but not why Gao wanted me to wait there. Once the trike was with the mechanic, it made no sense for one of us to stay.

The trike didn't even end up being fixed at that shop. The guy spent a long time running tests, only to conclude he didn't have the right parts. So, at noon we dragged the thing to Liyuan East Inner Market where there was another, bigger shop. Business there was good, and there was a line, so we went to eat lunch first and only waited a short while for our turn when we came back.

But this shop couldn't do the job either. Something about the part that was needed not being universal. S Company used Zongshen brand trikes, and we would have to order a replacement straight from the manufacturer. It was four or five o'clock by now, and I had wasted most of the day, with no hope of repairing the trike, and Gao wouldn't finish his deliveries in time to pick me up. I told him the situation, and he asked if I would push the trike from the market back to the depot. It took me almost an hour.

I also worked the next two days for nothing. Gao seemed to really depend on me. There wasn't a day he hadn't messaged for help. He must have thought I could be trusted, me being older than him. Or he didn't get along with the rest of the team and preferred a newcomer at his side.

To work more efficiently, we split up: I filled a sack with parcels and rode a shared bike with it slung over my shoulder, while he drove on the trike to take care of another spot. We met up when we were done.

With Gao needing my assistance all of the time, I naturally assumed that I would stay in his team once I had officially onboarded. I was already starting to get to know the area and my colleagues there, which would only make the work easier. But this is not what happened. The trial allocation had been random, and I wasn't assigned to his team afterward.

"You'll be working for free, for now, then," said one guy in the team, when he heard my situation. It confounded me.

This was a team leader. Let me explain: These so-called leaders were not leaders in any official capacity, and the role came with no benefits. In most cases, it was filled by the longest-standing member, who was responsible for keeping the workload even across the team and acting as the go-between with the depot staff. The reason they were willing to do these extra tasks without remuneration was that they had already secured themselves the best neighborhoods in their area. So, either they earned more than their colleagues or they had the easiest time—or they had found the ideal balance between the two. This same leader, who'd told me to work unpaid, said that this is what he had done for ten or so days when he first started, because no one had let him know about onboarding or that he wouldn't earn a *fen* until he had spoken to the manager.

He told me a day later that he worshiped President W, the head of S Company, because every Spring Festival the president selected the hundred best frontline workers out of four hundred thousand nationally, and flew them on chartered planes to headquarters for the New Year's party. He longed to be picked one year. He wore such a sincere and hopeful expression when he said this that I didn't know how to respond or what to talk about with him. The rest of the team didn't really seem to like him anyway, so I did my best to steer clear.

When Gao texted once more, the following morning, to see if I would join him on his rounds, it was with a proletarian sensibility that I replied, saying something had come up and I couldn't help him out anymore. I stayed in for two days instead, cooking and cleaning, going out only to do the groceries.

Then it was April 2. I started the day at the Linhe depot where I requested a signed employee registration form from Manager Z. At one o'clock in the afternoon, I then went to the Yunjing depot to find Director L. But he wasn't in his office. Stuck on the door was a notice: "Onboarding from 2 P.M. onwards."

The door of the neighboring conference room was open, so I sat in there while I waited. A succession of other applicants started to arrive soon after. Everyone eyed each other curiously, then turned their attention to their cell phones. No one spoke. At close to three o'clock, or maybe already past, Director L strolled into his office chatting with two assistants. They had just gone for lunch. One of the assistants, a woman, was a financial administrator who was also responsible for onboarding us. While she had been all smiles and chitchat with her colleagues, her face hardened the moment she saw us waiting. She made no effort to hide her contempt.

When it was my turn, she checked the system using the documents I handed over, but she couldn't find my name there. Apparently, Manager Z had given me an onboarding form but failed to submit the application for me in the HR system. She told me to talk with Manager Z again, then she scanned my documents while she had them at hand. Doing so, she saw that in my blood test report there was a note about my "neutrophil count" being marginally above normal.

"You failed your physical," she said, pointing at the report, without a flicker of emotion. "We can't hire you."

I hurried straight from the office to the hospital. The physical examination department was in a standalone building behind the outpatient department. I went inside and found an on-duty doctor. "Why is my rate for this outside the normal range, but it's written in the report summary that everything is fine?" I asked.

The doctor looked over the report. "S Company turned you down because of this?" he responded in a surprised tone.

Yes, I said.

"But this doesn't affect anything," he said. "The count fluctuates even if a healthy person just has some slight inflammation somewhere. It will return to normal after a few days. Turning you away for this is ridiculous." He repeated that last word several times while shaking his head, "ridiculous," but whether it was truly ridiculous or he was only trying to console the angry-looking man in front of him, I couldn't be sure.

"Can you change it for me, since it's normal?" I asked.

"I can't do that," he answered, without pause for thought. "There are rules."

"Then what am I supposed to do?"

"You will have to have another blood test," he said.

But it would cost money to have another test. "Will the result be the same, though?" I asked.

I didn't need to worry about that, he replied quickly. He guaranteed me it would be fine. This was a strange thing to say, I thought at the time. How could he guarantee this? What if there was still inflammation somewhere? But I listened to his advice and went for a second blood test the following morning, because what else was I going to do? Then I headed back to Linhe depot. Manager Z was out, so I asked the only assistant there if she would register my name in the onboarding system.

My test results came back the same afternoon and, sure enough, I was all clear. I realized I hadn't needed to wait three days for the report the first time around. The blood work was the only item on the form that supposedly took a little longer to complete. Even if they'd taken my blood in the afternoon, I should have had the results by the morning. This extra test had cost me another fifty yuan. Maybe the young courier was telling the truth when he warned me that there was something off about this clinic.

On the morning of April 4, I made my third trip to Director L's office. This time, the scowling finance clerk was on leave and unable to onboard me, so Director L told me to come back another day.

Fresh to Beijing and still jobless, I had a lot of free time on my hands, and I spent my evenings keeping a simple diary. All

I really recorded over those days were the journeys I had made, rather than any of my thoughts or feelings. Rereading the entry for this particular day now, I don't recall what came over me, but I ignored what L had said, and went to the Linhe depot to speak with Manager Z. Generally, I rarely disregard others' advice. But I probably didn't trust L anymore, by that point.

It was a half-hour walk between the depots. When I found Z, he told me that if I was in a hurry, I could try onboarding at the company HQ. S Company's Beijing headquarters were located in an Airport Logistics Park in Shunyi District, twenty miles from Liyuan. I left right away but still didn't arrive until the afternoon. The HR staff there were all young and well-mannered and, unlike the depot staff, highly educated. They gave me a very warm welcome. This was the first place where I got the impression that S Company was a modern operation.

They asked me why I had traveled all the way there for onboarding. I said that the assistant in Liyuan wasn't at work today. "Her again," one of them mumbled. It seemed that the assistant often took leave. They then discovered that the admin at Linhe depot hadn't sent in the scans of my ID, so they couldn't complete the process.

I contacted her. "There's no reason that I wouldn't have submitted them," she replied on the call, "I definitely sent them over yesterday." The HR staff checked again and worked out she had emailed my documents to one of the team's individual addresses instead of the team inbox like she was supposed to. I took out my ID and asked them to scan it then and there. They told me that I needed to have my ID verified at the public security bureau first, and confirmation wouldn't come back the same day. It was the Qingming Festival tomorrow, and then it was the weekend, which meant I had to wait three more days.

I was in my head the whole way home about whether these hurdles were just a streak of particularly bad luck, or if there was someone—Director L, for example—who was orchestrating them. Given my sour mood, I was leaning towards it being the director.

Half a month had passed since I first went to Yizhuang for the trial, on March 20. For all that time, I had been genuine about wanting to join S Company and hadn't looked for any other job. I had paid out of my own pocket for the physical examinations and worked a whole week for free. I was desperate, at least, to see some returns on my sacrifices.

Gao reached out, on one of those days, because he'd heard that I was having problems. He told me I simply shouldn't bother with onboarding. He had to go to his hometown for a while, he wasn't sure for how long, and he couldn't take more than three consecutive days' leave. He wanted to know if I would use his employee number and fill in for him in the meantime, and he would reimburse me directly. I could also stay on when he returned, if I liked. He could take on two more neighborhoods and let me make the deliveries, both of us under his employee number.

I turned down such a dishonest proposal, of course. There were people at his depot who did work like this, but they had a trike, and I didn't. He hadn't been able to hold on to the spare one he had borrowed. Basically, he hadn't fully thought it through.

On the afternoon of April 8, after the Qingming Festival, I went back to the second-floor office of the Yunjing depot. Like previously, Director L and the two assistants returned from their lunch at three. I was the only person there for processing today. The finance clerk explained again that there were no more openings, so if I still wanted to onboard, I would have to swap quotas. This meant waiting another day. Faced with her impatient, flinty expression, I didn't dare ask what the different quotas meant. I later learned that she was referring to the spaces for official employees being full, so while I could register as a contract worker for the time being, I had to wait for a space to open up to go on the regular payroll.

Contract workers had no base salary or benefits, and the company didn't provide them with insurance. In most cases, they were only responsible for delivering parcels, and didn't do collections. For each delivery they earned a 2.2-yuan commission, while employees received only 1.6 yuan, but this was on top of a base salary and benefits. There was also an extra 0.2-yuan fee for every couple pounds that a parcel weighed over the initial two. Certain special circumstances, like cash on delivery purchases made through teleshopping channels, also accrued additional commission.

Since the original registration form was now invalid, I went in search of Manager Z again the following morning. When I arrived at Linhe depot, someone told me he had gone to Yunjing for some business and would be back around noon. Wasting time sitting around waiting didn't appeal, so I hurried over to catch him. I found Director L's office door locked, and the floor apparently empty. One of the warehouse workers downstairs told me that L didn't usually turn up at the office so early. There being nothing more I could do, I went home to distract myself for a while, before heading right back at eleven o'clock and, this time, bumping into Z.

"What are you doing here?" he said. "Go wait for me in Linhe."

If you hadn't messed me around for the past two weeks, do you think I would be pestering you so much, I wanted to scream.

I finally got my hands on the onboarding form for contract workers from Z that afternoon. The assistant wasn't in again, but I was used to this by now and would avoid seeing her if I could, anyway. I traveled the two hours to HQ and the staff there, at last, onboarded me.

While they processed my registration, there was an overweight fellow ahead of me in the line, who was back after leaving the job once before. He must have weighed more than two hundred pounds. The office staff looked at his physical exam report and immediately pointed out that his blood fat levels were high.

Frowning, one of the employees asked him, "Did you leave to go and get fat?"

Everyone around us laughed. The man's face flushed red, as he struggled to think of a response.

"Get a friend to do the test for you," someone else in the line recommended. The office employee, who was well within earshot, didn't even blink an eye.

Roaming

The Linhe depot had sixty-plus couriers split into a dozen teams. I didn't have my own trike when I started, since the onboarding process was delayed so much that the depot's allotment of vehicles had already been distributed. There was someone else who joined at the same time whose hometown friend, who had recommended him, had made sure to reserve him a trike in advance. But I knew nobody at the company. There were three people in the whole depot without a vehicle, and I was one of them. The other two had been onboarded only a few days earlier than me and had already been given teams; I wasn't at that stage yet, and all the teams were full.

For the next two weeks, I began every morning waiting at the depot for Manager Z to assign me whichever team was down a member that day, and to slot me in. If nobody was away, then he slipped me in anywhere.

This nightmare arrangement made the work into an ordeal. With my own trike, I might have been able to work quite efficiently, but without one I became a burden to any team I joined. They could always have dropped me in a neighborhood and made me walk between addresses, only that way I could never have worked as quickly as the rest of them. Some packages were also too large for me to carry on my own, so I had to leave any over a certain size to the other members. Covering a different neighborhood every day like this, I couldn't streamline the work. Some apartment blocks weren't even numbered on Gaode Maps, and in those I just had to keep stopping people to ask for directions, which sometimes were wrong. For other neighborhoods, Gaode Maps showed the building numbers but not the shortcuts or side gates, so I invariably wound up taking the long way around to reach places. My colleagues didn't have the time or energy to give me the insider tips for every address—I might not even be with them tomorrow. This was why they sometimes ended up driving me from building to building. I was limited by my dependence on them and, at the same time, limited in how much help I could give. Having finished my trial, I wasn't even working for free anymore; the commission for any parcels they dropped me off to deliver was mine. It wasn't hard to imagine what some of them thought of me.

This wasn't always the case, though. There was one peculiar team that had only two members in total, as well as a domain so small that, were there any more of them, they each would have earned too little to make a living. Still, the neighboring teams for some reason refused to cede any territory, which would have allowed the duo to take on more people. The two workers could basically never have a day off—it was day in, day out for them. If they did, their colleague wouldn't have been able to handle the doubled workload. But sometimes this situation just couldn't be avoided. I remember when one of the pair was suddenly struck down with paronychia and couldn't work for several days. His teammate was very pleased to see me when I arrived to help out.

In that period I spent roving about, I covered nearly the whole domain collectively worked by the dozen teams of the Linhe depot: from the easternmost Seventy-Ninety neighborhood in Qiaozhuang to the westernmost building number 25 next to the Sinopec gas station in Jiukeshu; from the southernmost Xinqiao Garden in Tuqiao to the south side of West Yunhe Avenue to the north.

Eventually, one of the younger colleagues I worked with, by the name of Fei, decided to take me on. Unlike the others, he didn't mind about slashing his commission, so we became temporary partners, me riding on the back of his trike every day to deliver parcels with him.

Fei said he had started his first jobs when he was very young, building mountain tunnels and laying roads. After that, he kept livestock. I remember him mentioning donkeys at some point, which for some reason I thought meant he'd know something about horses: Were they difficult to look after? Expensive? He sneered that horses were no way to make money. But then neither was raising donkeys, he said.

There was one day that we saw pigeons in a cage on a balcony, and he said he used to keep the birds himself. Racing pigeons cost several thousand yuan apiece, and tens of thousands if from good stock. It gradually became clear to me just how interested he still was in the breeding industry, though there was a chance he only really wanted to earn back his failed investments.

That stretch of time working alongside Fei was relatively easy, but I made no money. Fei preferred to muddle along than to get anything considerable done. April in Beijing is when the Chinese mahogany start to bud, and he drove me all over the area picking the shoots. What I found strange was that there were mahogany trees growing in lots of the neighborhoods in Liyuan, but the buds still cost more than ten yuan per pound in the local markets.

Fei had a way with people, a knack for striking up conversations. Once, when we saw an elderly couple using a sickle attached to the end of a stick to hook the buds, he walked over and started chatting with them. The couple was very friendly, and it wasn't long before Fei summoned up the courage to ask for some. They were happy to oblige. But collecting them like this far from satisfied his appetite, so when he came across a tree he liked the look of, he would just climb up to pick a bunch.

Although Fei had been at S Company for half a year, he was still a contract worker like me, so he could deliver parcels but not collect them. The other four members of his team were official employees, even though two of them had joined even later than he did. But Fei seemed to have no interest in becoming an employee. He liked the freedom of contract work, he said.

When the company had increased our commission to three yuan per parcel during the last Spring Festival, so contract workers would stick around and work overtime while everyone else left Beijing for the holiday, Fei had managed to make more money than any one courier on the regular payroll, a fact that seemed to please him to no end and only cemented his decision not to sign on full-time.

There was one day further down the line when we ditched work together because he wanted to stroll around the animal and flower market in Qiaozhuang. It had rained earlier in the day, it was chilly out, and our destination looked like a mudflat, with standing water and sludge all over the ground, and several electric pylons looming nearby. The so-called animal and flower market was really nothing more than a few rows of spaced-out stores with a line of vendors' stalls down one side. It was a dreary place, all in all, though this might have been because it was a weekday.

Fei had been there before and knew it well, first leading me around the stalls selling bonsai. At one, he wanted to buy some seedlings, but he and the vendor couldn't agree on a price. Next, we went to a pet stall, I thought because he assumed I preferred cats and dogs to plants.

Then he spotted a store selling pet turtles and started negotiating with the owner, a man in his fifties, who couldn't have cared less about our patronage. The turtles were in cardboard boxes lined up outside the storefront. Fei had a mature alligator snapping turtle at home, and he had come to the market to find a friend for it. He only told me later that this had been the point of the whole trip.

He reached down and pinched the tail of one of the bigger turtles, lifting all of what must have been at least eight pounds of it to show me how to differentiate the sex by inspecting its anus. The turtle looked fierce. Spikes studded its skin and shell, and it had a mouth like an eagle's beak—sharp and merciless. But it turned out to be a docile creature, and it put up no fight.

The owner stood off to the side watching us, doing nothing to intervene—neither to push the sale nor to shout, like I worried he might, "You touch, you buy!"

I didn't know at the time that Fei was really going to buy it, and I knew nothing about snapping turtles, especially not that there are "real" alligator snapping turtles and "fake" common snapping turtles. I can still picture the scene of him dangling the turtle by its tail, when he turned to me and confirmed that it was a particularly hefty common snapping turtle. He gave nothing away though, acting like he was just asking random questions. He even fooled me. But the turtle must have been proving difficult to sell, because the owner reluctantly made him an offer.

After paying, Fei and I cut back to the bonsai seller, with him carrying the turtle in its box. Although we had already walked away once, the seller would not budge from his original price, and we left without making another purchase.

Once I started to feel at home in Fei's neighborhoods, he seemed to become even lazier than he already was. Come lunchtime, he would say he had to go home for some reason or other and leave me his trike to finish the afternoon deliveries. To be fair, two of us using the one trike can't have been that much more efficient than only one of us, so he really was just committing to earning less while he spent more time with his feet up, not that he had been especially industrious in the first place. He was good to me, though, looking back. He might have loved to show off, which made him seem insincere, but he meant well.

There wasn't one occasion I can think of where he tried to take advantage of me, and I never lost out or felt inconvenienced by him. His interest in looking after plants and animals was genuine too, it wasn't just about investment—he really enjoyed it.

We were making a delivery in the courtyard of an old dormitory once, and he pointed at what looked like a chicken coop in the surrounding wall. "There's a stray cat living in there," he said, stopping the trike. He climbed off, then went over to the hole and started imitating a cat's call to try to lure it out.

It was a shame that I later changed teams and had less opportunity to see him. Later still, when I moved to another company, we gradually stopped talking on WeChat. He still reposts S Company ads on his Moments page now, one every few days, so he hasn't given up drifting about on his S Company trike all this time later.

It was another couple of weeks before I was finally allotted my own delivery trike. I had to collect it myself and drive it the more than twenty miles back from Shunyi. I picked it up at a place called Tianlong Auto Parts City, on the side of the sixth ring road, where there was a sea of cars but not a person in sight.

Auto Parts City had closed down, but the bus station still had the same name. S Company had rented an outdoor space there for storing scrap vehicles. Looking over at them, all I saw was a jumbled array of trikes and bikes, a few hundred at least, and most of them in dire states.

Three young guys greeted me. They were mechanics. Two of them looked like minors, and the other can't have been much older. They were wearing vests and shorts, and were covered with grease and grime. "These have all been fixed. You can pick yours from there," said one of them, pointing at some vehicles nearby. I turned to see which they were referring to and was instantly disappointed. They were in a sorry condition, with a whole range of obvious problems: doors that wouldn't shut properly, or holes in the roofs that let in light and most definitely rain. They were filthy as well, like they had never been washed before, but it was the damage to their bodies and the missing parts that really struck me. The wheels on one of them were different diameters, so it stood lopsided. That these vehicles could get moving at all seemed a miracle in itself. It made me consider the three young mechanics with brand-new respect.

The trike that Fei had been given after onboarding looked untouched compared with these, even though he had already driven it for six months. I had gotten used to riding Fei's trike, and now I had to lump for one of these beat-up old things. I felt let down. But I'm a firm believer in making the most of any situation, and I knew it was my fault for having such high expectations in the first place.

Choosing one of the vehicles was like trying to select the cookie that got least dirty when someone dropped the whole bag on the floor. Once I'd picked one, the mechanics fitted the battery, then a lock, and handed me the key. That was when I noticed that the battery wasn't lithium, but lead-acid. Lead-acid batteries are heavy things. Two of them weigh more than sixty pounds altogether. I lived on the sixth floor, with no elevator, and from then on, I had to carry both up the stairs every evening for charging and down again in the mornings.

I drove back to the depot that afternoon and was immediately dispatched to Tuqiao to lend a hand. Once I reached Xinqiao Garden, I reversed the bike, which suddenly cut out and wouldn't start again. I pushed it to the roadside repair shop opposite Huayuan Wonderland neighborhood, working up quite a sweat because of the parcels in the trailer and the slope of the road.

The repair shop was run by a small man who was both the owner and the self-assured technician. "The controller is broken. You'll have to replace it," he told me, without room for question. The trike hadn't even earned me a *fen* yet, and I was forking out 150 yuan for it.

When I saw them later my colleagues said, "You've been ripped off. There was probably some problem with the circuit connections." I had thought as much myself when the guy said that the controller was faulty: If he knew the wiring was the issue, was he more likely to connect it up properly for me and take my 10 yuan, or tell me the controller was broken and take 150? Since I had already swapped the controllers, I decided I was better off believing him. After all, he might have been honest.

That evening, when I pulled up on the trike in front of my apartment building for the first time, I realized I finally felt settled: My job was stable.

Joining a Team

Soon after getting my trike, I officially joined a team that covered a stretch of neighborhoods in Yirui East, to the south of Tuqiao subway station. I took care of two neighborhoods there, Gaoloujin and New Town Leju, as well as the nearby Universal Studios construction site. The worksite was enormous, 1.5 square miles it said online, with a perimeter fence the whole way around and more than twenty gates. I was responsible for main gate number three opposite New Town Leju, on the south side of Qunfang South.

Gate three didn't get many parcels really, only ten to twenty on most days, but boy, were they a pain to deliver. I wasn't permitted to enter the site, and there was no parcel locker where I could leave them, so the only thing to do was to wait outside. I tried asking the security guards to take them, but they weren't associated with the various construction units that managed the different sections of the site, and refused.

Lots of the people who were waiting for parcels had no form of transport. They walked to collect their deliveries, which took twenty or so minutes, and they often took their sweet time—at least that's how it seemed to me.

There were some who were truly busy, though, and couldn't just drop everything in order to come meet me. Like the tower crane driver who had a penchant for online shopping. I would call his cell, and he would apologize that he was otherwise occupied midair and couldn't make it down right then.

Could I bring the parcel tomorrow, he'd ask.

But he would also be in the sky the next day, so we'd push to the day after.

In the end, it would take several trips to deliver a single parcel. But this didn't dampen his passion for online shopping.

It became more of an issue by the summer, when mere moments after parking my trike outside main gate three the metal would be scalding hot to the touch and I would end up soaked with sweat from only making a dozen phone calls. I usually went there twice a day and often had to wait more than half an hour each time. Some people never even showed, despite me calling them repeatedly to hurry up. Soon, soon, they'd say, but they were only stalling for time—it wasn't soon at all. Sometimes I had been gone for an hour already before they would finally call back, "I'm outside, why can't I see you?"

Gaoloujin was always my first stop of the day. After I left the depot, it took approximately twenty minutes to get there. It was a resettlement neighborhood, meaning that half of the people who lived in Gaoloujin were resettled farming folk from when the urban expansion had subsumed their home region. Inside the main gate, to the right, there was a five-meter-wide, three-meter-high screen that was showing the daily headlines when I drove by on my trike every morning. I supposed this was the new era of the open-air film viewings that were once so common in the countryside.

When there was a death among this community, the immediate family would put up a temporary mourning hall so wider family and friends could offer their condolences. These mourning halls were colorful, and not the black and white I had imagined; the frame, covered with a water-resistant canvas, was forty or so meters long, around three meters tall, and four meters wide, with a decorative *pailou* arch in the entranceway that could also be taken down when no longer needed. My first time seeing one of these halls, I thought it was a tent for promotional activities for some electrical appliances company.

Gaoloujin had sixteen buildings in total, with numbers one through seven reserved for resettled residents, and numbers eight through sixteen for tenants from elsewhere. Deliveries to the first seven were easy, since the elderly members of families were always at home throughout the day. Even if I happened to turn up when they were out doing the groceries, they were happy for me to leave parcels by doors or inside the utilities boxes. The residents were so close and looked out for each other so well, in fact, that no one even dared to paste up small ads in the neighborhood, for fear they'd be caught by the senior citizens.

The tenants, by comparison, were a mixed bunch. Most of them were migrant workers, young drifters, and then some co-renters. They were all out at work during the day. None of them knew their neighbors, and with lots of strangers going in and out of the building it was easy for parcels to go missing. When I first started with the team, a colleague put me on buildings eight to sixteen, while he did numbers one to seven. Every day I tackled half of Gaoloujin, the whole of New Town Leju, plus the Universal Studios construction site. Constantly rushing back and forth between them left me feeling spent and defeated.

Gradually, I slipped into a pit of negative emotions at work. While some neighborhoods were good to deliver to, others weren't, and when people took the good addresses, the rest of us were lumped with the bad ones. It was like a zero-sum game between colleagues; inevitably someone lost out. Everybody worked the worst neighborhoods early on, and some people left as a result. Those who didn't might eventually move on to covering a marginally better spot and, if they outstayed everyone else, maybe on to the best ones. But this always left the undesirable areas to the new arrivals. Newbies rarely argued, though, they just took time to cotton on to the inherent injustice at play, usually a month or two, but sometimes not even that. Everyone surely had a limit to how long they would wait for a "promotion" before they moved on. What this meant was that half the team was unshakeable, and the other half was like a revolving door.

I had no interest in falling out with my partner and bargaining with him at every turn. But neither did I want to work with someone who was going to take advantage. Imagine finishing later than a colleague every day yet earning less than them—of course I was going to feel irritated and dissatisfied, and at some point, I would stop really caring about the job. There is a reason that deep-sea fish are blind, and animals in the desert tolerant of thirst—a big part of who I am is determined by my environment and not my nature.

At that point I had already started to notice how my work situation was changing me, little by little, making me irritable, prone to anger, unconcerned by my responsibilities. I felt no longer capable of meeting the expectations I had of myself, and I didn't really want to try to, either.

There were changes I noticed that occasionally thrilled me, though, and in those impassioned moments my despondency and restlessness fell away. Like the time I cursed out a woman I didn't even know—I rarely ever shout, which is why this has stuck with me.

Usually, when any of us left a trike to drop off a delivery, we left the key in the ignition, so as not to waste time inserting and removing it hundreds of times a day. No one in the neighborhoods was going to steal a courier vehicle.

One day I was carrying a box of parcels upstairs, and I had just reached the second floor of the block when I glanced out of the hallway window and saw a woman, she might have been fifty or sixty years old, who had lifted a toddler onto my trike's seat to play. The grandchild had his hands on the handlebars as if he was driving. If he had only twisted the accelerator ever so slightly, the trike would have started moving. I dropped the box in a panic and raced down the stairs.

A colleague of mine had recently forgotten to put on his trike's hand brake while he went inside one building, and the wind had blown the trike into a roll, right into a sedan, scraping its side. He ended up forking out 1,600 yuan to compensate the owner. I didn't dare to imagine the damage a toddler on a trike might cause—or the injuries. He could crash into the sedan parked in front of it, which I couldn't afford to pay for—or he might hit a passerby—or even worse, he might fall off the seat himself and be run over by the wheels . . . I almost blacked out just thinking this.

I was fuming when I reached the woman and started yelling. She just looked at me, shamefaced. "Children are silly, yes, but grown-ups too?" I still remember shouting this at her—it's a line that I heard the actor Ge You say once in a film.

Paying for damages was all in a day's work for some couriers. Most of the time it was for lost parcels, but there were other circumstances. One younger Yunda Express delivery guy, who was driving around Gaoloujin too quickly on his trike, had to swerve to avoid a pregnant woman and fell off, smashing the windscreen. He didn't hit the woman, but he gave her a fright. He paid almost two thousand yuan to repair the trike and compensate the woman. I can still picture his wide-eyed look of panic as he told me after the fact, "I quit." He seemed no less in shock than the woman must have been.

The largest sum I've heard of being offered as a settlement also happens to come from the most bizarre incident I know of, which unfolded in the Fangheng Eastview neighborhood on Linhe Road. A courier shoved a parcel inside a fire hydrant, breaking the water pipe or connector and sending water spraying into a nearby elevator shaft, ruining the electrics. It cost him thirty thousand yuan.

Fortunately, I had been lucky in my first six months with S Company. I hadn't lost any parcels and I hadn't had to pay out for anything. There was only really one incident, when I was delivering a parcel of fresh fruit, express, to an apartment. When I knocked, a woman's voice shouted for me to leave it outside in the corridor. This was nothing unusual. Some people wanted to make sure they were holding their pet before opening the door, and some women who lived alone would avoid answering at all if it was a stranger outside. They would wait until I left to collect the parcel. I could understand this, of course, even if I wasn't wholly convinced that someone would be so bold as to commit a crime in broad daylight in Gaoloujin.

Anyway, I put the parcel down and left, only for the woman to call a short while later to say she had to decline receipt. I explained that she had already accepted the parcel when she told me to leave it outside her door, and now that I had updated the system, the process wasn't reversible—parcels that had been accepted could not then be rejected.

"How could it be so user-unfriendly?" she asked. "It's only been two minutes, can you not change it?"

"There's nothing I can do after even a second has passed, never mind two minutes," I replied. "If you think you might not want it, you must check the product while I'm there. You asked me to leave the parcel. How do I know you haven't opened it yet?" Plus, the part I didn't say out loud: And we're not talking two minutes anymore, that was more than twenty minutes ago!

Hearing my response, she started to act dumb, questioning how I could accept the parcel in her place when she didn't check it herself, and so on. I was angry by now. This woman was being so difficult and unreasonable, going back on her word and contradicting herself. I found myself despising her, suddenly. It wasn't worth arguing with this sort of person. So, I spent my own money—some tens of yuan, I've forgotten how much exactly, but the box of fruit weighed around six pounds—and helped her to return the parcel to the sender. When I went to collect the fruit, she had placed it back outside her apartment, but I could see that the box had been opened then resealed. I hadn't laid eyes on this woman the whole time, but she had swindled me out of thirty, forty, or fifty yuan, and was still thinking that the person outside was a bad person she needed to protect herself from. I didn't know what I was supposed to say to somebody like that.

There was another time when I made a seventy-year-old man wait on the sidewalk for almost three hours. Afterward, I was shocked to discover that I didn't feel the slightest bit guilty.

Many customers preferred not to provide a complete address on the delivery form. They had their reasons, but it only made my job more difficult. I had one form once that didn't include a building or door number, only that it was for the Gaoloujin neighborhood. I called ahead to find out where to go, and the recipient said he didn't live in Gaoloujin at all, he just went to the market there every day for his vegetables. He was about to step out of the door, he said, and would be there in half an hour. Could I wait for him?

I had a full load of parcels still to deliver and couldn't waste five minutes, never mind half an hour. I told him to phone when he arrived. Then I went into the neighborhood complex and, moments later, totally forgot about the whole thing.

The customer never called me, either. I finished my morning deliveries and was about to leave to collect the next batch, when an elderly man by the market shouted for me to stop. He had glasses on and a head of gray hair. "Young one, are you from S Company?" he asked.

"Yes," I said.

I knew right away who he was. I quickly rummaged about in the back of the trike for his parcel and handed it over, at which he responded quite angrily, "I've been waiting here for you all morning, why didn't you wait for me?"

I flinched in surprise: He had been standing there for nearly three hours. "Why didn't you call?" I asked.

"I did, nothing went through," he said.

It was true. My cell wasn't easy to get ahold of. There was no signal in any of the elevators in Gaoloujin or in most of the corridors. When I phoned him that morning, I'd been on the road on my trike. The traffic and my anxiety had probably contributed to me not sounding particularly friendly. It also irked me when people didn't give their full address—if they valued their privacy so much, they shouldn't use express couriers. But I hadn't known that the customer was so elderly. I explained to him how many parcels I had to deliver every day and how I had to keep moving if I had any hope of getting through them all. I couldn't sit around waiting for people.

Perhaps he hadn't heard me properly, but he just kept piling on the criticism: "It's not proper, working like that. The customer is king, do you not understand?"

I balked, then instinctively became defensive. "But there should only be one king. I have to serve hundreds every day."

At this, he laughed. He hadn't been angry at all; he was just having some fun. He had a wicked sense of humor, it turned out. He shook the little box at me and said in a low voice, "My wife doesn't let me buy them, so I don't let you deliver them to my door."

Orders from teleshopping channels were also a regular nuisance: Customers who had bought clothes would want to try them on when they first arrived and sometimes canceled the order on the spot afterward, in which case we didn't receive a *fen* of commission. We stood there twiddling our thumbs for who knows how long, just wasting our time, and it was us who inevitably had to fold the clothes and repackage them. One customer even opened and pulled out their electric tea kettle only to decide they didn't want it. I had to re-insert each of the dozen or so components into the precisely shaped shock-absorbing packaging by myself. It took me half an hour to work out where they all fitted. We all loathed teleshopping purchases.

One parcel I remember was for an older woman in Gaoloujin who was very kind to me. She had bought a robot for learning English as a present for her grandson. She wanted to open it to test it, but didn't understand how to work the thing, so I read the instructions while explaining to her what to do, though this wasn't really my job.

The robot, from its packaging to the instructions to the product itself, was very shoddy. I got the impression it was a knockoff from the markets of Shenzhen that should have cost no more than three or four hundred yuan, but the receipt said that the woman had paid more than two thousand. I could tell that she wasn't happy with the robot either, but her biggest concerns were that the robot was too small and didn't look like it had on TV. The product was obviously a rip-off, but I was only there to deliver the parcel, so I tried to reassure her, "With gadgets like this, it isn't the bigger, the better. Sometimes the really tiny ones are more valuable."

But she was clearly still unsure. She asked me to wait a moment, then took out her cell phone and dialed the customer service number. No one answered. But as soon as she hung up, her cell started ringing. I was standing next to her and could see the screen. The number that was phoning had automatically been identified as a "spam caller." When she answered, I could hear a customer service voice on the other end persistently trying to coax her into completing the purchase, saying that if after use there happened to be any issues, she could call the service line again for information, and if she still wasn't satisfied, she could then return the product.

The call had clearly done nothing to ease her worries, but she must have decided to take pity on me, noticing the beads of sweat on my forehead. "I'll pay you first, and if there are any issues, I can contact customer service," she said. I felt terrible, though I couldn't say why. There was no mistaking that she was in a more stable financial situation than I was. But this wasn't to do with the money, even if money was a regular concern of mine.

"Customer service won't be as patient with you after you've paid," I managed to build up the courage to say. She looked taken aback, probably assessing my motive. "I don't think this robot is worth two thousand," I continued.

"I don't think it is either," she said, "but I don't want you to have wasted a journey."

"Don't worry about it," I said. "I only deliver the parcels. If you pay, the money doesn't go to me anyway." If she had pressed confirm on the order, I would have earned a whopping 0.2 percent commission. It wasn't worth the nightmares I'd still be having years later if I didn't say anything.

For logistics and couriering, the slack season lasted from the start of the year until autumn. According to Manager Z, this extended low period was for training the troops to be ready for battle in the peak times. He was a military veteran, and the so-called training he went on about was just listening to his lectures. He loved holding forth—and avoided individual conversations at all costs—yet he never enunciated clearly enough for me, standing at the back of the ranks, to make out what he was saying.

Eager to load our trikes and start our rounds in the mornings as soon as the trucks had been emptied, we first had to endure one of his rousing speeches before we could set off. He invariably gave these, with an august look on his face, in a serious tone, but he never actually said all that much. He simply repeated the same things every day, things like: "You have to do what I say!" "If you want to do this, then do it well. If you don't, then get lost!" "S Company will survive without you or me, but if you leave S Company, you'll struggle at every step!" "There's nothing special about you, but S Company has given you the platform for there to be!" "Are you the ones who pull in customers? No, the platform tells you the deliveries you must make!" "Don't think we can't do this without you, anyone could do this!"

Essentially, he wanted to beat into us that we owed our every success to the success of the company. We were only cogs in a machine, and could be swapped out at any moment. He obviously incorporated some army rhetoric, too, it was just that any allegiance was to S Company rather than to the Motherland.

And these were only the morning meetings, which didn't seem to satisfy his intense need for enterprising spirit. So, every week, we had two to three evening meetings. For those, we had to wait until every courier had finished their deliveries, all the returned parcels were loaded onto the truck, and the depot was spotless. Only then would he start, by which time it was often past nine. These meetings went on for so long that we sometimes didn't adjourn until after 11 P.M.

I still attended every single one in my first two months there, even though I couldn't see the slightest significance in them. They only guaranteed zero free time for relaxation after work and zero remuneration for listening. Contract workers' commission was calculated per parcel we delivered, and we received no benefits or welfare—it was unreasonable of the depot to force us to join. But Manager Z clearly saw things differently. On those days, he would remind everyone on WeChat repeatedly, to the extent that I didn't dare to skip. The evening meetings were intended to instill discipline, I realized, with Manager Z singling out anyone who had made a mistake for public humiliation.

I remember one evening when I turned up at the depot after the meeting had already started, because I had clocked off early and gone home to eat dinner. I saw Manager Z shouting a stream of invective at everybody. He had picked a number of colleagues to do pushups as punishment for something. One of the team, though, refused to abide this sort of management approach and began to argue back. He looked like he might even become aggressive. This same colleague had recently lost a parcel and had been made to pay out three thousand yuan, so it was easy to imagine his state of mind.

Arriving late to this scene, I felt even less inclined to join and, fortunately, no one had noticed me yet. But I knew if I started reversing my trike, it would automatically blare, "Vehicle reversing, caution." I couldn't shut it off. So as not to give away my movements, I tiptoed back to my trike and wheeled it backward out of the depot yard. I still felt on edge when I finally made it home.

The colleague who had the disagreement with Manager Z was transferred the very next day to a neighboring depot. I never saw him again. I didn't attend any more evening meetings either, but luckily for me I was never found out. They could fire me if they wanted, I thought, but I wasn't going to let them humiliate me. From an objective standpoint, unconventional methods like this must have done a good job of weeding out disobedient, lax employees. S Company didn't need to dismiss them, because they left of their own accord, which meant it had no obligation to pay them a single *fen* of severance. The people who remained were fairly compliant and kindhearted, or they were at least resilient.

Sick Leave and Temporary Transfer

I had long known that S Company had a good reputation, as the "Haidilao of couriers." But Manager Z reminding us in meetings that we should help customers by taking out their trash seemed a bit much. I never asked anyone if they wanted that particular service, but I was more than happy to oblige the one customer who suggested, unprompted, that I empty their bins.

Manager Z also demanded that we invite customers to award us a five-star rating after every successful delivery. There was a table that showed our employee stats stuck up in the depot. On it, they updated our daily ratings, and the lower-ranked colleagues would be singled out during meetings.

This was a real cause of distress for me. Not a day went by where I didn't feel anxious. For one, I was afraid that I would end up at the bottom of the table if I didn't do these extras, but I couldn't even bring myself to open my mouth in front of customers. Instead, I resorted to compiling text messages on my cell at the end of a shift, requesting that the customers I had served that day give me a good review. I handpicked those who had been especially polite or warm toward me, and I excluded any elderly folk, since they might have struggled with the technology even if they had been willing to help. I sent twenty to thirty of these messages a day; I found doing it this way much easier than in person.

Frequently, there were customers who praised me to my face. Some even praised S Company's service: "It's much better than those whatsit-TOs." It made me feel awkward every time. I had always envied the "whatsit-TOs"—their parcel deliverers only had to deliver parcels, there was none of this meeting malarkey, taking out customers' trash, asking for reviews, and they weren't at risk of getting complaints on account of the slightest slip-up.

The July temperature in Beijing was easily over ninety-five degrees. With no AC in my apartment, I regularly woke up in the middle of the night, completely damp with sweat. This lack of rest, and the fact I didn't allow myself to drink water on shift because of how hard it could be to find a restroom—or the time to use one—must have been a big part of the reason I caught a cold despite the season, a cold I couldn't shake for far too long.

June and July are slow months for logistics, so two of the longer-standing team members took extended vacations to go home, which left me unable to arrange any time off for two consecutive months.

I wasn't concerned, at first. I had had colds before and just taken ibuprofen, and all was well. But this time there was no sign of improvement for a whole two weeks.

To keep me going, I popped an ibuprofen before I left for work every morning, until one lunchtime I almost fainted from the heat. My head felt like it was going to explode, my ears ringing inexplicably. I checked my temperature when I got home. I was running a fever of 103.46 degrees. I messaged in the team WeChat group right away to request sick leave. First thing the next day, I went to Luhe Hospital flu clinic.

There, my temperature reading had dropped to 101.84 degrees, maybe as a result of the ibuprofen. The doctor asked me how long I had been sick.

Almost three weeks, I told her.

She asked if I had taken my temperature at home, and what was the highest it reached.

It had reached 103.46 degrees, last night.

Her response was the quietest "fuck" I had ever heard. Then she printed a form and sent me straight for a CT scan.

The diagnosis was viral pneumonia. The doctor told me to get IV treatment for a week, then return for a checkup. However, since I was still a contract worker and S Company didn't cover my medical insurance, it would cost me fifty yuan just for the registration fee, every day that I went to Luhe Hospital for liquids. If you asked me, this didn't add up. I didn't need to consult a doctor each time I came for a drip, so why did I have to register more than once?

I asked if the illness might pass on its own. The doctor shot me a look that said something along the lines of, You're not a child anymore, how can you still be so ignorant? Only, what came out of her mouth was that it wouldn't.

"But," she continued, softer now, "you can take your IV prescription to a smaller clinic if you prefer."

Right, I was only getting an IV, I could go anywhere for it. Why drain the resources of a top-tier medical establishment? So, I rode a shared bike to a community hospital I found on

Gaode Maps, located on Qunfang Middle First Street, close to where I lived. Nobody could sniff at my determination to save money, which was still strong even though I was as sick as a dog.

I noticed the IV room by the entrance as soon as I arrived. Behind a glass wall sat a row of elderly people with drips in their arms. I had come to the right place, I told myself, this was their specialty.

But the physician there took one look at my prescription and said, "This is for an anti-inflammatory. We can't provide that here." This seemed odd; why would they turn away business? But I didn't feel like investigating. I left, scanned another shared bike, and luckily found another small clinic nearby, on Qunfang Middle Second Street.

Business didn't look to be going well for this clinic. There was one doctor and no nurses or patients. The doctor must also have been the owner, watching the place by herself. Again, she hesitated on seeing my prescription. She asked if I had pneumonia. When I said I did, she muttered something that I couldn't make out. I didn't push her to repeat it. I felt too weak to argue with her. All I wanted was a clear answer. Eventually, she begrudgingly agreed to give me the IV. But now it was my turn to have misgivings. The attitudes I had come up against in both clinics so far had made me wary. Why were they being so difficult? Were there risks involved with administering the anti-inflammatory that they were unequipped for? I was having second thoughts. This was also when I became conscious of the clinic being pocket-sized. It wasn't laid out like a medical center at all but more like a massage treatment clinic. There were even diagrams on the walls showing the acupressure points of the body, and I'm a skeptic to say the least. I believe in Western medicine and its doctors. After some hemming and hawing, I made my excuses and headed back to Luhe Hospital.

I missed a week of work because of this sickness, every day of which I spent going to the hospital for IVs and sleeping through the afternoon. By day eight, I felt like I had fully recovered, so I didn't go back for a follow-up as instructed. I was afraid the doctor would want to do another CT scan. The first one had cost me three hundred yuan. I did the calculations later and worked out that, considering the missed days of work, this single period of illness set me back some three thousand yuan, which was what I earned in half a month.

The depot pulled in staff from other teams for support while I was off. This happened occasionally. I had helped out the two-person team myself when I was healthy. Once, I helped out after a reshuffle that briefly left a new young worker on his own. I think I was sent to fill in because I'd done a few days in the area before, but this didn't mean I was confident I knew the beat.

This new guy was called Ma. How long we worked together I can't remember now, but I do know that on the evening of the last day the two of us had a disagreement. It was over something very basic. As a contract worker still, my job entailed only delivering the parcels, whereas he also had to collect them. So, naturally, his was the larger workload. Not to mention, I was only there as support—I wasn't one of his team—and I was well within my rights, in my eyes, to leave once I'd completed my assignment of deliveries. But Ma worked slowly. He was either still getting to know the area or he was just slow. Regardless, he struggled to manage. When I finished up each evening, he would still have a pile of parcels to deliver. In the first few days, I stuck around to help him out, even though it meant working in the dark in old residential areas I wasn't familiar with, like Yuqiao Nanli North, where the buildings were all run-down six-story blocks and the streetlamps did very little. Just making out the property numbers was a challenge, so dropping off a few additional parcels wound up being unnecessarily complicated. It was a lot of extra work for barely any extra pay.

Ma was obviously of the opinion that, since I had been sent in as reinforcement, I was his temporary partner, and I ought to do as he did; that I had a duty to the team that extended beyond my own assignment of packages. But I had a bellyful of gripes about S Company at this point, and was nowhere near as assiduous in my duties as when I first started. I had had too much rotten luck: the two weeks wasted over delayed onboarding; the lack of a trike early on and how tiring and unprofitable this made the daily grind; being assigned to a team late, and to an awkward area for deliveries; the great big hole that having no insurance had burned in my pocket when I got sick . . . all experiences that had damaged my initial resolve, to the extent I refused to take the same responsibility for the team as Ma. I was only there as a short-term helper. And I had helped him, on a number of occasions, but I couldn't keep doing it forever. I wanted to go home at a reasonable time—not that it was ever early anymore when I finally managed to leave—and I didn't intend to keep forging on with him by the light of the stars.

On that last night, after clearing the remaining parcels that had piled up, I decided I had had enough. I told him I wouldn't be coming the next day, and I didn't care what they said at the depot. I'd run out of patience. I put in a request for leave that evening, because in his team if you didn't take vacation, you never got a break. It was almost a month since my last day off, and that was before I'd even been transferred to his team. I explained to Manager Z that there was some personal matter I needed to attend to.

With me not at work, the depot had to assign someone else to support the small team. That someone was a new recruit by the name of Yan, from Shanxi. I imagine this was because recent hires tended to be more eager to muck in than long-standing employees. Yan happened to have been working with Fei up until then, and so referred to me as his *shixiong*—his fellow student under our *shifu*, Fei—even though we had never actually been partnered. Unfortunately, his first day helping Ma turned into a bit of a disaster.

Being brand-new to the company, and still learning the ropes, he understandably felt very anxious about suddenly having to cope in an unfamiliar location. To make matters worse, Ma, who was struggling to manage himself, didn't have time to even show him around. So, on the first morning, Yan couldn't find the right entrance to the residential complex and, as a result, had delivered only a dozen parcels by noon. There had been no need for Ma to give me the tour when I filled in, since I had previously done some rounds in the area. Plus, I had experience jumping between different teams, so I wasn't easily rattled. But Yan didn't even know how to use Gaode Maps and just wandered the streets, searching for locations with his eyes—which was, of course, never going to work. Beijing is a little more complex than a field and a few fences.

Come the afternoon, Ma called me to say the young Yan wasn't up to the task and asked if I could help. I said I was unavailable. Later, the depot also called to see if I was free. I told them I wasn't in Beijing. By then, I had grown cold-hearted—no one could change my mind.

How they eventually resolved the issue I never asked. They probably dragged in another unfortunate soul as backup. I couldn't have cared less. After my period of leave, I went straight back to my own team without consulting anyone. No one made it into a problem, though, so I got away with it. It turned out that people only bullied those who seemed weak and were afraid of anyone who stood up for themselves.

Yan quit after no time at all. He must have been struggling to adapt. His health was bad. Apparently, he had coughed up blood one day. He was also short, under five foot, and found it difficult to lift the larger parcels down from the roof of the trike. He went back to Shanxi and started a property management job in Taiyuan, with a salary of just over a thousand yuan a month. We stayed in touch on WeChat, and he asked me if there were any vacancies I could refer him for. He still wanted to come back to Beijing. But he couldn't be a courier, and I didn't know anything else.

Peak Season and Jumping Ship

Come September, S Company's preparations began for the upcoming peak season. These started with a team building meeting at the depot, at which everyone tucked in to watermelon and drank soda. Director L came along to play host and motivate. He made us stand in two separate groups at either end of the depot depending on if we had joined before or after the 2018 Spring Festival; two-thirds of the room ended up on the same side as me. Which meant that the majority of employees at the depot had only worked there for a handful of months. One of the longer-time couriers joked on the down-low that the leadership loved to whip us into doing our jobs in the less-busy times, but when the sales came around, they were on their knees begging for us to stay. It was also the only time when we could request change of any sort, and they would respond promptly.

Two weeks later, the couriers from the three depots around Liyuan all dined together at Harbin's Only Farmhouse Food on Tongma Road. The meal ended up being quite the feast. I'd say it was the best I had eaten since moving to Beijing. Having always lived in the south, I had no idea that northeastern food could taste so good. Coated in thick and rich layers of starchy velveting, the sweet and oily dishes shimmered gold and wholly sated my long-starved appetite. I don't think people realized what a free meal meant to me then, given I wasn't usually a picky eater. I wolfed down whatever was placed in front of me, until I could barely move, and still the waiters kept the dishes coming. There was also unlimited beer and *erguotou* spirit. I was too overwhelmed to speak. I'd been given a pass to a lavish buffet when times were hard—that was how it felt. I only wish we had sat down earlier than 10 P.M., so I could have stayed longer, but we had to be up for work the next morning. This meal was by far the highlight of my six months at S Company.

Another interesting thing that happened around then was I got a call from Fei. I was at Gaoloujin, and he said he was coming to see me. This seemed strange. He covered the strip around Gebudian South, and I was miles away in Yirui East. Why would he travel all that way for me? But he had always been so laid-back that I figured he just didn't want to work that day and wanted to catch up instead. Which is pretty much how it worked out; we chatted while he watched me do my deliveries. "Are you hoping to get a transfer to my team?" I asked, eventually. He wasn't, he said. He was there to see me, that was all. As I came out of one apartment block he even handed over a soda he had bought for me, as if he was still every bit the top dog between us. After hanging around for an hour, he headed off, leaving me baffled.

I later heard that he had finally gone too far with the slacking, and this visit was him being made an example of. The depot could track the live data on how much work we did, and there was no room for dead weight. He might not have been interested in earning more money, but the company wouldn't stand for its valuable resources and space being wasted. With peak season approaching, steps were being taken to deal with low-efficiency workers. Leadership had ordered him to observe how I went about my rounds, since among the contract workers my level of performance was consistently quite high. Obviously, this was embarrassing for him—he had been my mentor, after all—but this was exactly what the higher-ups hoped. They wanted to shame him into working harder.

For the imminent battle that was Singles' Day, the depot was allotted a new quota for official positions. Before it hired anyone new, it had to make a portion of the contract workforce into actual employees. For this, it gave a compulsory promotion to each of the four drivers that ranked highest in terms of delivery numbers. I came fourth. But I had no intention of signing on as an official employee. The one employee that had been in my team had already quit, and I planned to do the same very soon. To earn even the base salary in the area we had been assigned to was beyond exhausting. I also didn't know how long I would have to keep working those neighborhoods before I would be transferred to a better beat.

I had been planning to leave since my bout of pneumonia. But I couldn't go until I found my next boss. There were a few options: A courier at YTO Express had told me that he made six thousand–plus per month during the down season and clocked off at about seven every day. "I might as well give it a try," he said.

A Cainiao Logistics station in Gaoloujin had headhunted me to be the courier for three buildings. The work was easy and included two daily meals and a guaranteed base rate of five thousand yuan, but I would have to load up in the evenings, which meant not finishing until after half past ten.

Lastly, a courier at Pinjun Express had tried to recruit me, saying they earned around six thousand a month in the quiet periods, did short days, and like with S Company, the depots nationwide were chains rather than franchises. The company also provided full insurance coverage and always paid wages on time.

I had been dithering about making a decision while I looked around for something better, but S Company insisting that I take a promotion forced my hand. The company wanted me to become an official employee, but also to continue doing deliveries in Gaoloujin. Essentially, it wanted me to replace my colleague who quit, the same colleague who had complained constantly about the work. I'd understood his plight as well, but I felt no pity. I was in the same position he was; maybe even a worse one. Becoming the next him was definitely not the plan. But quitting when he did was a bold choice.

An army takes a thousand days to train to be ready for battle on a single morning—this was one of Manager Z's favorite messages to us all. The "morning" in question was in fact two days: Double Eleven and Double Twelve (November 11 and December 12, respectively), the peak times in logistics. I had listened to Manager L's attempts to rouse his troops, had eaten more than my fill in the mess, and now I planned to desert my comrades in arms with the battle looming on the horizon.

But before I did, Manager Z was dismissed himself. I presume the depot's numbers had become abysmal under him and the higher-ups had lost confidence that he was the right general to lead the troops into Double Eleven. He joined JD.com shortly after, where he still is today, which I know through his occasional posts on WeChat.

When I told Director L of my decision, he looked irritated. "Just as you're about to start earning real money, you're going to give up?" It wasn't hard for me to imagine that this only cemented his initial impression of me that I wouldn't last long at S Company. But who could blame him for being annoyed? He had just told me I was being given official employment and I was thanking him by saying no thank you.

The nerves I felt when I saw that he wasn't happy took me right back to six months earlier, when I had come asking for a job. Only, he hadn't wanted me back then, whereas now he didn't want to see me go. I really wasn't having a good time at S Company, though. I tried asking anyway if I could change zones as an employee, even if I already knew the answer—of course not. Enough people requested transfers that, if leadership green-lighted every single one, there would be nobody covering the less desirable areas.

Still, I felt like a sham. I didn't want him thinking that this was the reason I was leaving, so I made up the excuse that my parents were getting on and needed me around to care for them, which was why I was swapping to a job with shorter hours. S Company was asking too much of people, I had to leave my place at six in the morning to get to work on time, and couldn't go home until past eleven at night because of the meetings. There was no need for it.

Director L probably figured out that my parents weren't in Beijing, but he didn't say so. I never told him I had already found another job, of course. He certainly wouldn't have been pleased then.

The day I processed my resignation I met with the mean-looking finance admin once more, and she seemed even less happy to see me than the first time. Us couriers coming and going so frequently must have been wearing at her like the tide on a beach; we had to be a major source of hassle. But I was delighted. I would never have to see her again.

Once I had left, I received a care text message from the S Company HR department. The system had sent it automatically, no doubt; every courier who left received one. The message expressed both thanks and regret, and also inquired whether I had found a better opportunity elsewhere. If so, it requested that I share the particulars with S Company, to give it a chance to secure me an equivalent arrangement. I knew that this was only talk, a sales pitch, but I remember thinking that they got the wording just right—I should have saved what they wrote, I realize now—and gave a convincing impression of a company that looked after and valued its employees. I was curious whether the copywriter who had composed the message was still employed at S Company when it reached my phone, and whether when writing the message, they had even believed it themselves.

The New Post

I'm generally not someone who likes to complain, or even talk if I can help it, but I still used to snipe at the company on occasion with fellow colleagues.

When I bumped into the other couriers who worked my neighborhoods, in the elevator maybe, our usual conversation was moaning about our respective employers. Not that we were especially unhappy or anything, it was just reliable common ground. It won us each other's trust and warmed us to each other. We built our friendships in opposition to this shared enemy.

Small talk was all it was, really, something to say to be polite, like when Beijingers ask if you've eaten. But it was thanks to this idle chatter that someone, knowing my grievances with S Company, referred me for a new job.

Everything worked out. Or maybe I had low standards. Anyway, in September, I left S Company for Pinjun Express. The non-franchised companies, like Pinjun and S Company, and also D Company, JD.com, and TMall Distributions (which later became Danniao Logistics), were the only ones that bought full coverage for their couriers, and after my brush with pneumonia I felt like medical insurance might be useful; if I'd been insured back then I'd have saved myself some money. Plus, I'd been put off the five main state-run companies by word they often delayed payments. They were STO Express, YTO Express, ZTO Express, BEST Express, and Yunda Express—or the "Big Five." I didn't want to take that risk.

Fewer people will have heard of Pinjun Express, but the company wasn't so different from JD.com; it was Vipshop's dedicated logistics company, mostly handling order fulfilment and returns collection, while also operating a more routine courier business. The company's Liyuan depot was by the main gate for Golden Bridge Era Park on Yunjing South Avenue, even closer to my place than the S Company one.

M was the depot lead there, a young man on the chubby side who looked a little like the Laughing Buddha. His eyes even crinkled when he smiled. He was very welcoming and answered all my questions, even making the effort to keep the conversation going when I had nothing more I wanted to ask. Our introduction couldn't have been more different from my first meeting with Manager Z. M helped me to fill in my onboarding form without me asking him to. He told me to write in the "Previous Occupation(s)" section "agricultural work," even though I had an urban residency permit and no land to farm.

"You can't put that you worked for S Company," he instructed, "or else they'll ask to see a certificate."

The onboarding process took place at Pinjun HQ in Majuqiao Logistics Park, which was twenty kilometers away despite still being part of Tongzhou District. There I underwent a day of training, mostly introductions to the company culture, job norms, and regulations. In the afternoon there was an easy written test that pretty much everyone passed—it was a formality, really. And that was everything. I couldn't stop wondering afterward why there had been so many hurdles at S Company when Pinjun made the whole process so smooth. What made it so that the Pinjun depot lead was genuinely interested in competence and commitment, while the S Company leadership seemed totally aloof and difficult? There were probably lots of factors, I realize, some of which I've already mentioned. But there's one more thing that I think only becomes apparent through comparison.

S Company, being the bellwether of the industry, enjoyed a surplus of human resources and very advantageous labor-management dynamics. The low-level administrators in the company—whose domain was reality and not the utopia of corporate social responsibility its claims suggested—used the company's enviable position to enforce more thorough appraisals. The result was, Director L and Manager Z's sense of entitlement made it difficult for me to meet their standards. Pinjun Express, meanwhile, didn't have the same weight in the labor market that big players like Meituan, Ele.me, S Company, and JD.com used to push staff around. So, the management assumed a humbler manner with regards to its employees. Or, put another way, us workers could speak up more, were actually listened to, and the work atmosphere was freer, all of this without us having to forgo the salary paid by S Company.

I've always been someone who acts on their own initiative. I'm not a draft animal, I don't like to labor under the crack of a bullwhip. Pretty quickly, it became obvious that Pinjun was a better fit for me than S Company. When I told my new colleagues that I'd had to attend regular meetings in the evenings at my former job, which sometimes didn't end until after 11 P.M., they all looked at me sympathetically.

Pinjun's Liyuan depot had a total of eight staff. Depot lead M managed three depots and didn't spend much time at ours. His role was similar to Director L's. The daily manager at our depot had a deputy position and, like us, had a regular assignment of parcels to deliver. My colleagues were very young and got along really well from the looks of them. Since Pinjun's shifts ended quite early, everybody had time to hang around awhile at the depot after, playing games on their cell phones or chatting. It can be a highly effective stress-relief method for couriers to be able to bellyache together about the company and the system, the place, and the clients. This was also a chance for us all to share stories about the oddball customers we had encountered or funny experiences we'd had. When I joined there was still more than a month to go before Singles' Day on November 11, which thankfully gave me time to familiarize myself with the new work environment and adjust my working methods appropriately.

S Company's parcel assignments had been much less concentrated than I knew those of the Big Five were, but Pinjun's parcels were even more spread out than that. Most neighborhoods received only a dozen or so parcels daily, and some only a handful, so we each worked across a very wide area. The territory I took on included eight residential complexes, two shopping malls, two office buildings, and two business venture parks. I could even apply to cover more if I wanted to up my earnings. Basically, working for Pinjun required a different set of tactics than the one I'd used at S Company, a more efficient approach. But I wasn't aware of this when I started. Since the busy period hadn't arrived yet, I was able to briefly get away with the same methods I was used to and still easily complete any given day's tasks.

Jade Orchid Bay was one of the neighborhoods I was responsible for. It was where I spent most of every day, since most parcels went there. But the largest number of parcels was still only around twenty. There were twelve buildings in the high-class neighborhood altogether, joined by lots of greenery—trees, flowers, lawns—rock arrangements, watercourses, mini bridges, and pavilions. The neighborhood covered a very large area.

It was a really beautiful place for the people living there, with all the birdsong and the smells of flowers and the winding, secluded pathways. But for couriers, it was a nightmare: The paths were all very circuitous, and there was hardly a straight road in the whole place; sometimes, just to get from one building to another required taking a long roundabout route. Plus, couriers were not allowed to enter the complex on their vehicles. I had to pull a trolley loaded up with parcels instead, which meant working slowly. A recipient who wasn't in when I arrived might ask me over the phone to leave their parcel in the locker by the neighborhood's gate, and then call again before I left to ask, "Sir, where did you leave my parcel? I haven't received a code."

"I'm still in the neighborhood. Please be patient a moment longer."

"In that case, bring it up to me. I'm home now." Typically, this happened just as I was about to reach the gate. Backtracking specially for one customer would waste a lot of precious time, and I didn't really want to, but I didn't know how to say no.

I made it about a week before a concerned-looking deputy found me for a word. "Singles' Day is coming up. Then Double

Twelve. You're going to be handling double the number of parcels every day. You're already so stretched, how are you going to manage the increase?"

This was the first I was hearing there was an issue. I didn't feel stretched at all. I had gotten used to working until 7 or 8 P.M. every day at S Company, and now that I was finishing before six, I almost felt guilty. But he had reason to worry—as things stood, if my workload doubled, I would be done for. I did want to know how my colleagues were so efficient at completing their assignments, so I ran through my day with him, and when I got to what happened at Jade Orchid Bay, he cut me off. "You should never go back. If a customer asks for a second attempt at delivery, then you do it the next day."

"But he had me put it in the locker first, and I hadn't yet. He obviously guessed that I was still nearby. What excuse can I use to say no?" I asked.

"Tell him it's already in the locker but the text message with the code can take a moment. He can collect it once the code arrives." The deputy saying this sparked a lightbulb moment for me: While S Company demanded high-quality service, here they prioritized efficiency.

Reflecting on other situations I hadn't brought up, I managed to work out for myself an improved method for approaching them in the future. S Company's superior customer service was built on high costs and high prices. Jade Orchid Bay alone had three S Company delivery guys covering it, whereas I was ranging an area of several miles every day. There was no way I could be at people's beck and call. I especially couldn't backtrack. But this should have come as no surprise to customers paying Pinjun Express's lower fees, though apparently it still did.

I got to know one of the S Company guys who worked in Jade Orchid Bay soon after this. We both started at S Company at around the same time but belonged to different depots. Jade Orchid Bay was a bum deal for S Company couriers, worse even than Gaoloujin had been for me. With a place of that size prohibiting trikes from entering, the company had resorted to assigning three couriers to the one neighborhood in order to guarantee the prompt delivery of parcels. There being more of them certainly shortened response times, but each courier only covered four buildings, limiting their income. He told me that his salary after tax was not even five thousand yuan, and it wouldn't increase unless he changed neighborhoods. But he was the least-experienced member of his team. Even if an opportunity to swap came along, it wouldn't be his to take. He didn't know how long he would have to stick it out.

Chatting one day, he started to talk about a parcel that went missing after the client had told him to leave it by their door. The client had come home expecting to see the parcel outside and it hadn't been there. Fortunately, he kept the voice messages as proof of the client's request, and he had taken three photos of the parcel on the doorstep as further evidence of his innocence. He was proud of this level of foresight, but it all seemed ridiculous to me. "You have to take pictures every time a customer asks you to leave a parcel outside?" I asked. He said he did it without fail. "You make one point six yuan for every parcel you deliver, and that includes making a phone call, sending voice messages, taking photos. Is it worth it?"

This comment wasn't really directed at him, but at my former employer. When I had been at S Company, Manager Z used to say, "Here at S Company we want customers to sign for every parcel. If a customer asks you to leave their delivery by the door, or with the store downstairs, or beside a fire hydrant, or in the entranceway or utilities box, and the parcel goes missing, then you'll be the ones who must pay. The company won't be held accountable." Yet there was an incident when a colleague from the nearby Yangzhuang depot asked a customer to sign for receipt and the customer had refused to. Maybe they had been in a bad mood, or just thought that having to sign was overkill, but when the colleague insisted, the customer complained that he "had a foul attitude." The company took the complaint on board, and Yangzhuang punished him with three days' suspension, which he had to spend going from one neighboring depot to another to read aloud his own letter of self-criticism.

The morning he finished reading it for us during our depot meeting, Manager Z asked everybody, "Who thinks this was unfair?"

"I do," we all replied at once.

"I think it was justified," said Z. "Customers of the Big Five pay ten yuan for a parcel. They pay twenty-three with S Company. Do you still think it's unfair?"

Nobody answered. The twenty-three yuan didn't go to us. We made only 1.6 yuan from it, which was about the same as couriers at the Big Five.

We put up with this sort of talking down to us every day at S Company, so much so that I started to think the industry was totally backward. So many of those working in it were outright uncivilized. Bullying and deception were standard fare. But having left S Company, I could see that this might not be the universal experience. I had just been unlucky.

The young courier heard what I had to say, and his face dropped. He didn't speak, but I could see he resented what I'd suggested. His attitude towards me changed that day. He stopped greeting me with a smile when we saw each other, and he didn't banter with me like he had anymore. He just looked sullen.

Not a month later, his colleague told me he had quit. The parcel that went missing had been found. A garbage collector had taken it thinking it was an empty cardboard box. But the neighborhood security guard recognized the person on the CCTV footage and managed to chase the parcel down shortly after.

Time Cost

I don't know if anyone really likes delivering parcels, deep down. If they do, they're a rare breed. Anyway, myself and the other couriers I knew didn't. Payday was the only time when I felt like the work I had put in was worthwhile. Not when a customer looked grateful or said thanks—although I appreciated these gestures.

I did some calculations: The couriers and food deliverers in our area, whose pay package didn't include food and accommodation, earned on average seven thousand yuan a month. This was determined by the cost of living in Beijing and the strength of their work. It was a market shaped over many years. Anything lower than this, and the workforce would have headed elsewhere, to other areas or other industries.

This amount, based on me working twenty-six days out of the month, represented a daily pay of 270 yuan. This was the value of my work—I'm avoiding calling it "my price." I worked eleven hours a day, spending one hour unloading the truck, sorting the parcels, and loading my trike, then another hour altogether on the road traveling between the various neighborhoods. Those were my fixed costs. They dictated that, in the remaining nine hours I spent making deliveries, I had to earn 30 yuan every hour to reach my desired wage. That's 0.5 yuan a minute. Flipped, this was my time cost. Each completed delivery earned me an average of 2 yuan, which meant I had to complete a delivery every four minutes in order not to run at a loss. If that became unworkable, I would have to consider a change of job.

Slowly, I got used to approaching all questions from a purely financial standpoint and only looking at time from the perspective of cost. For example, if a minute was worth 0.5 yuan, then the cost of urination was 1 yuan—that is, if the toilet was free to use and I only took two minutes. Eating lunch needed twenty minutes—ten minutes of which were spent waiting for the food—and had a time cost of 10 yuan. If a simple dish of rice and meat cost 15 yuan on top of this, then the whole endeavor was too extravagant! Basically, I skipped a lot of lunches. I also hardly drank any water in the mornings to reduce the frequency of restroom breaks throughout the day. When delivering parcels, if the recipient wasn't home—which was half of residents during work hours—besides the 0.1 yuan fee it cost to make a phone call to them, I also incurred a 0.5 yuan time cost. If the recipient asked for the parcel to be left in a locker, then the time cost was even greater—around 0.4 yuan per parcel—so I lost out in that transaction. If they asked me to come back another day, then we were in dire straits—I'd not only spent time making the phone call, but I also now had to work double the time for a single delivery.

These numbers were only when the tasks went smoothly: If the recipient didn't pick up, I had wasted a minute waiting for nothing, a minute that still cost me 0.5 yuan. Or a call might be impossible to put down, once it got through, if the client insisted on making all sorts of unmeetable requests. There were occasions when I had already incurred a time cost in excess of the commission after only a single call, and I was still yet to deliver the parcel.

Like the time, in Jade Orchid Bay again, I went to pick up at an agreed time a Vipshop parcel that a customer was returning. But the customer wasn't in. When I called, a friendly, middle-aged-sounding woman's voice told me she would be home at seven o'clock. Would I come back then, she asked.

Since I finished work before seven, I requested to swap the delivery day for tomorrow. But she wouldn't be home until seven tomorrow either, she said, it was the same every day.

"If that's the case, I suggest you take the parcel to your place of work to return it," I said.

But she worked at a hospital, she replied, and it was inconvenient to attend to personal matters while there.

I explained that her only option was to post the parcel back herself, since Vipshop's pick-up service didn't support evening appointments.

This was a pain, according to her. S Company was the only other courier service that offered pickups in Jade Orchid Bay, but S Company's fee was higher than the ten yuan the platform would reimburse for return deliveries. It was why most people didn't like to use S Company. She also didn't want to have to take the parcel to a depot herself, which she would have to do if she went with another company. She might not be able to find the place—or she just couldn't be bothered. Calling on me to do her dirty work for her was much less trouble. Eager communicator that she seemed, I got the impression she was someone who believed most things were possible if only you fought for them.

After I turned down her various suggestions, she asked if I couldn't come back to Jade Orchid Bay for an evening stroll once I'd finished work and my dinner, and collect the parcel while I was passing by. With the way she spoke—her attitude, tone, diction, not to mention her charm—I couldn't fault her. However, an evening trip to her neighborhood wouldn't be as idyllic as she was making it out to be. It was a one-hour return journey, during which I'd have to endure traffic and car horns and exhaust fumes and traffic lights . . . Who was going to choose an evening stroll like that over relaxing at home with their family?

Then there were the financial implications to consider: Making an extra trip for her one order was bad math. We earned 3.5 yuan commission for accepting a collection. I obviously didn't intend to spend an hour of my time for all of 3.5 yuan, especially not when it was overtime. There is a good chance that she was the kind of workaholic who was happily duty bound to make sacrifices for her job, and in this intensely competitive society she naturally assumed that I would be the same. But my being less enlightened than her, the suggestion that occurred to me was: Why don't you take an after-dinner walk yourself? And stop by a depot while you're at it! I didn't actually say this, of course, I just came up with an excuse to refuse. I made several deliveries to her after that, and she was very polite in person, as well. She clearly bore me no grudge for having said no, or if she did, I didn't notice.

One thing I know for certain is, I didn't suddenly start bringing in the big bucks once I became, suddenly, painfully aware that time is money. In fact, the basic patterns of my work didn't really change. I didn't throw all caution to the wind and start putting every parcel into the lockers, and I didn't stop picking up phone calls or simply blocking unknown numbers—it was like I now cared and didn't care about money, at the same time. I often envied the young couriers for the Big Five who, in more than half of our Liyuan neighborhoods, no longer went inside buildings. They deposited parcels directly into the lockers, or their company rented a space to serve as a drop-off point. Either way, the customer received a text telling them to fetch the parcel themself.

But I still liked Pinjun. It might have been a relatively small player in the industry, but it avoided a lot of messy labor-capital disputes by operating as a chain. It was also backed by Vipshop, which relieved some of the pressure of survival.

We did have to go to doors when delivering parcels, though, like with S Company. My method was different for every neighborhood. How it looked depended on the longstanding tacit agreement that existed between the residents and the couriers, which in turn depended on the practicalities of the neighborhood itself. Whenever I accepted a new neighborhood into my rounds, I first consulted the other couriers about how best to approach it, then tailored their advice to suit myself.

Obviously, some places were easier to run deliveries in than others. The worse places I thought of like this: I transferred onto them the time I saved in the good neighborhoods, as if it was a subsidy. So really, the residents there ought to have been thanking their counterparts in the less annoying neighborhoods.

Still, it quickly became apparent that many people had no clue about the working methods of couriers, even if they received and sent parcels almost every day. For me, most of these misunderstandings boiled down to a lack of insight into our means of remuneration. For instance, there was a store salesperson I had a parcel for, which was addressed to Jingtong Roosevelt Plaza, but she had been transferred to Wanda Plaza in Tongzhou and hadn't changed her delivery information. I told her over the phone that she would have to wait until the following day for the parcel to be redirected to her new place of work. It would no longer be me delivering it, either, but that goes without saying.

She sounded surprised. "But it's so near. Why does it take a whole day? Can you not just drop it off here in a moment?" She was far from the only customer who had asked me this question. In fact, she wasn't even in the minority. It got me thinking that certain things I consider to be common sense just don't even occur to others. And with those people, patience is essential.

First of all, Roosevelt Plaza to Wanda Plaza was not the jaunt around the corner that her casual tone implied. Even on a fully charged trike, it would take half an hour minimum.

How you view this prospect really depends on who you are. For a young woman promenading the streets on her day off, no two malls in the city were too far apart. But for couriers like us who might spend most of their day rushing around one or two neighborhoods, whether it's a few miles to a mall or twenty miles to Tiananmen Square it's all equally out of reach.

Finally, Wanda Plaza was enormous, and was a place I hardly knew. Finding a specific store in there could take forever. A mall didn't need to be all that large for me to easily lose my way trying to navigate it.

None of this should have been particularly difficult for her to imagine, if only she had been willing to put herself in my position. But I preferred to give her the benefit of the doubt rather than believe she'd demand I go out of my way especially for her, if all I got out of it was a measly two yuan. She simply must have thought I earned more.

My area of responsibility included two malls, both next to Jiukeshu subway station. Jingtong Roosevelt Plaza was one, and the other was Sunshine New Life Plaza. People mostly referred to the latter as, simply, Carrefour, even though the hypermarket only occupied the second and third floor of the building. The official name just wasn't widely known. Couriers were not allowed inside the mall, having instead to stand by an entrance and call recipients to come collect their parcels. This suited couriers for the Big Five just fine—they didn't want to go inside anyway, and, in this case, customers couldn't argue with them when they didn't. They parked their vehicles and made one call after another, then sat there and waited. Meanwhile, I rarely had more than three or four parcels for Carrefour, with recipients that were invariably at work when I arrived, and couldn't come straight out. I wasn't going to waste thirty minutes waiting to make only a few deliveries, but I couldn't call ahead in case a customer came outside and I wasn't there yet. My solution was to go in myself, since I walked quicker than customers. But I didn't have to do this many times before I was caught by security.

The guard grabbed me by the exit for GOME Electrical Appliances on the fourth floor, right before I got to where I was going. "I only just started delivering here, I didn't know the rules," I told him. I knew them, really, but I didn't have to tell him that. "There's no sign at the main entrance that says couriers can't come in, and no one stopped me when I did. I'll just go now, how about that?" But he gripped the handles of my trolley even harder and wouldn't let go. "You won't let me in, and now you won't let me leave. What do you want to do?" I asked.

"I'm confiscating these parcels. You have to learn your lesson!" We were in a deadlock.

I insisted that I was ignorant, and I really was new—this was the first time we had run into each other. Other couriers had warned me about the ban, but he didn't know this. He hadn't told me off before, so he was in no position to say I needed to learn my lesson. Besides, I wasn't convinced that he could confiscate the parcels—in what land is that law? Threatening me, too, just seemed ridiculous. My transgression hadn't caused any actual damages, and I wasn't a shoplifter. Mine was a minor violation of rules made up by the mall. He didn't need to be eyeing me so hostilely. I decided not to buy into his misplaced self-importance.

"Let me go," I said. "You don't have the right to take my parcels." He mustn't have understood, or he simply didn't hear, because he only tightened his grip on my trolley. He was like a bulldog with its prey clamped between its jaws. "I'll call the police if you keep this up," I said.

"Go ahead if you want to," was his response. So, I took out my phone and dialed 110. If I remember rightly, that was the first time in my life calling the emergency line. The switchboard operator noted down my information, then told me to wait and a district officer would call back in a moment. I had to be sure to answer. Meanwhile, the security guard asked for his colleagues and supervisor via walkie-talkie. I was curious to see how much of a fuss he was prepared to kick up for so small a trifle.

His supervisor arrived and started talking like he was lecturing me. I pleaded again that I was new here, I didn't know. I also reaffirmed that the mall had no authority to take the parcels, so I had contacted the police. This guy was obviously sharper than his subordinate because, the moment he heard the word police, he must have weighed up the situation and decided it was best to back down.

He swore at me, to win back some face, then said, "Call 110 again and tell them the matter is resolved. You can leave with the parcels now, but you're not allowed back in."

I thought that would be the end of it, but there were still more twists and turns to come. The customer I was delivering to—a gym manager on the fourth floor—suddenly rushed over. I had just explained the situation to her on the phone, and the moment she saw the supervisor she started yelling. It was clear there was bad blood. She called him a scoundrel and a scumbag, and though her tone was nasty, as far as I could tell this wasn't overly harsh or even very far from the truth. The only difference between scoundrels and the guards was that the guards wore uniforms. This superior even had a large scar on his face, and he spoke and acted in a really rowdy way. It isn't good to judge people based on appearances, I know that, but I'll make a bold assumption that he wasn't always an honest person.

After the gym manager left, Scarface became irate at having been shouted at. "These parcels are staying here, I'm taking them. See what happens if she tries getting them back," he said, turning to me.

I had no choice but to go with him to the mall's central control room. I had to keep an eye on the parcels. The customer hadn't even signed for them yet, so I was still liable. This was when an officer from Jiukeshu Bureau called my cell. I explained what happened, and I could hear in his tone he was miffed that we were turning this into such a big thing. He asked where I was, then he phoned the control room landline. He already had the phone number. Scarface answered and maintained his tough tone throughout the conversation, only to agree to return the parcels the moment he hung up. But he wasn't going to give them to me directly, he said, I had to get the gym manager to come collect them, so she could write a letter of guarantee or an official report before he let them go. "But she hasn't even signed for the parcels yet," I said again.

"You sign for them," he said. "Bring her here and you won't have to worry. This is nothing to do with you."

Complaints and "Revenge"

Singles' Day arrived soon after—November 11, "Double Eleven."

I remember in the run-up to the "Big Push," so from the first of the month until the tenth, the number of parcels we were handling daily had gradually decreased, until eventually we could clock off by four or even three in the afternoon. It turned out that our customers cared far more about our platform's Big Push promotions than I'd expected, eagerly suppressing their retail appetites in order to fully indulge on the big day.

This stretch of more relaxed shifts became somehow oppressive. I spent every moment of it apprehensive about the storm that was about to come and could do nothing to prepare. I was of two minds about how I felt: hungry for the high yield the sales window would bring, but also worried about making mistakes. The truth of the matter was mistakes were inevitable during the Big Push. It was why the worry was winning out.

To ensure we didn't screw up during such a crucial period, the depot lead, M, posted daily reminders in the team WeChat group for us to check our trikes were working fine. Half of all repair costs would be reimbursed for a limited time only. But I couldn't find anything wrong with mine: The three tires were still pretty new, so I assumed the inner tubes were also okay. There was some wear on the brake pads, but nothing out of the ordinary; braking distance was just a little farther than it should be. The headlights still worked, too, even if they wouldn't for much longer. But I never went to get them repaired.

All this fretting and mental preparation, inversely, might have been the reason I didn't find the extra work as tiring as I'd thought it was going to be, once the promotional event got officially underway.

In the first four days, our workload tripled, then for the rest of the sales period it remained at a consistent two times the usual. But double the workload didn't mean spending double the time working, as my area didn't also increase commensurately in size. Only the density of deliveries rose. Whether I delivered three or ten parcels to customers in Jingtong Roosevelt Plaza, it took about the same time.

After we'd unloaded the truck in the mornings, we had to wade between the waist-high boxes that filled the depot to bursting point and even overflowed out the gate. I ate a quick breakfast at half past six, then had my second meal of the day at 9 P.M., but I never felt hungry. Maybe I was so focused on work that I didn't notice the pangs before they faded. My body's endocrine system automatically regulated itself as necessary, as if a laborer who meekly accepts their lot when a foreman refuses to compromise.

December ended up being the much tougher month. The days were shorter, for one, with the mornings staying dark until past seven and the sun going down before even five o'clock; it gave me the impression time was slipping away, which is guaranteed to cause anxiety. In winter our trike batteries could also carry us only a third of the way they did in summer. They became ticking time bombs that might leave us paralyzed on the ground at any moment. I don't think I'd worried about my batteries even once in the summer. But now I felt on edge every time I had to brake or restart the trike as I moved between neighborhood buildings, in case the engine suddenly decided to give out.

The temperatures in Beijing had dropped very low, sometimes staying below freezing for entire days. I had always thought I could stand long periods of cold and used to wear only jeans even in forty-one degrees. That was me for all of the winters in the south. But I had very little experience of weather in the twenties or lower. I have lived in five different cities, and only two of them ever got so cold: Shanghai and Beijing. I mostly worked indoors in Shanghai, and the temperature there dipped, at most, four or five degrees below freezing. In Beijing, I would head out in the mornings at 6 A.M. and start my days battling temperatures in the teens. I also had to work for long hours outside and could only use fingerless gloves because of how often I needed to use my cell phone. Luckily, the handlebar mitts I put on the trike were quite effective, but I would still end up with my hands frozen stiff on most days. I might struggle to even bend my fingers, never mind use my phone's touch screen.

Part of the issue was we couldn't wear too many layers, as it would hinder us when carrying parcels and climbing stairs. We didn't want to risk getting any expensive clothing dirty or damaged, either. Not that I owned any expensive clothing. My most pricey item must have been a pair of New Balance sneakers that cost two hundred and something yuan. Working in those every day, I wore through the soles after a year. In the low season, I walked between ten and fifteen thousand steps daily. In the high season, it was more like twenty thousand, and around Singles' Day and Double Twelve, thirty thousand. My step count wasn't even high compared with some of the colleagues I had on WeRun. I rarely even ranked in the top three.

In December and January, the coldest months, I wore thermal base layers, a wool sweater, and a zip-up vest, then on top of these, a medium-thick coat and a pair of icebreaker pants. If it ever became too cold for me to bear when I was on deliveries, I would take shelter in a hallway for a while to warm up. As reward for our suffering in December, myself and all my colleagues at the depot earned over ten thousand yuan each after tax.

I didn't go home for the Spring Festival in 2019. As an on-duty worker, I only had five days of vacation. Originally, the Vipshop stance was, "We never shut for Spring Festival," which is also what I told customers. But it didn't turn out this way in the end. The driver who dropped off the parcels at the depot in the mornings told me that nobody was working overtime for the few days of the holiday, so it was impossible to keep normal business operations going. No parcels could reach the depot. But there ended up being relatively few Spring Festival orders anyway, probably because brands had already sold out of the stock they wanted to clear, and the new lines weren't on sale yet, or they were but they weren't discounted, so customers wanted to wait until they could get more bang for their buck. I remember on the first day back at work sorting the parcels that had built up over the several days of the holiday, their number did not even reach what we usually handled in a single day.

After the Spring Festival I noticed that a few regular customers had disappeared. Either they had stopped using Vipshop, which was unlikely, or they had left Beijing. Quite a few I knew had just moved elsewhere in the city. I had to collect at least ten parcels in the following month that had been left at the wrong address, all because the recipients had forgotten to change their delivery information. These movers tended to have been co-tenants, whose old roommates had accepted their parcels for them, even signed for them. With the orders "fulfilled" in our system, I had to pay to redeliver the packages myself, unless I could get the customer to do it.

One time, I knocked on what I thought was a customer's door in LC International South, and nobody was in. When I called her, the customer made me leave the parcel in the utilities box right outside. She then phoned that evening to say she couldn't find the package. She had left the wrong address when she made the order, we realized, since she had now moved to Changping. On the phone earlier, she had thought I was outside her Changping place. "I can collect the parcel for you tomorrow and mail it on to Changping, but you'll have to pay the postage fee," I told her. She was very apologetic for the extra trouble she thought she'd caused, and quickly agreed. But people like her were few and far between. The majority weren't willing to reimburse me and would argue.

"You'll have to pay for the postage," I told another customer over the phone.

"Why?" he asked. "Shipping was included."

"You gave the wrong address," I said. "The parcel has already been signed for."

"By whom? I didn't receive it."

"I brought it to the address that you gave. The people living there now signed for it."

"But that's not me," he said.

"I don't know you," I said. "I only know the address you provided."

"Didn't you check?"

"I said your name to the person at the door. How else am I supposed to check?" Enough people in co-tenant situations didn't know the names of their roommates that it was common they would accept the parcel if the address was correct, then just leave it in the communal area. He obviously knew this; he just didn't want to pay eight yuan for his own mistake.

"I'll be contacting your customer service, then," he told me.

Negotiations usually fell apart at this point. I couldn't let him call customer service, so I had to cover the postage myself. It only cost eight yuan, sometimes ten, but boy, did people like him grind my gears. If he had been standing in front of me, there was a high possibility I would have slapped him.

I ran into a similar situation in Hongxiang 1979 Cultural and Creative Park. I arrived at the company address I'd been given, and called out the recipient's name, prompting a woman to leave the conversation she was in to come over and take the parcel. The recipient phoned the next day to ask where their parcel had gone. After I explained the situation to him, he started acting as if he'd done nothing wrong, grilling me sanctimoniously, "Are all you couriers this irresponsible? Don't you know to double-check?"

"I check the name for every parcel I deliver. Someone signed for you," I said.

"I don't know that woman. Why would she take the parcel for me?" he answered.

"If you don't know her, then why does it say her address on the order form?" I replied.

"It must have been wrong. But that isn't me. Didn't you check?"

To be honest, I didn't know what more I could have done to check. I had no authority to make people show identification, and why that woman took in a parcel for somebody whose name she can't have recognized beats me. Maybe she was new there and didn't know all her colleagues yet.

Even if I could check IDs, it was extra time spent for no extra income. I didn't earn much in the first place; any lower and I couldn't have put food on the table.

If he had only been willing to pay out a measly eight yuan to remedy his own mistake, then I would have gone to collect the parcel for him and sent it to the correct address. But I wasn't going to squabble. He was being an ass. Not only did he show zero remorse, he was being totally self-righteous, saying he too did manual labor and understood the plight, but one shouldn't be so slack about their work, that sort of thing—trying to tell me how to act. If I'd fought back, he would have submitted a complaint, and who knew how he might have distorted the facts talking with customer service. So, I collected the parcel and spent my own money to send it to his new address.

I also wrote his name, cell number, and address in my phone's notes. I was genuinely furious—in fact I exploded—but I had to swallow my anger for the time being. When I left, though, I told myself I would definitely go looking for him for payback. Revenge is a dish best served cold.

But in reality, I never went to find him. Of course I didn't. My anger subsided before long.

His was one of two names that ever made my "revenge list." I eventually deleted both, without having acted on either.

I was chatting with colleagues at the depot one day when one of them mentioned that they knew a courier who had banged up an Audi. The Audi driver had been beeping his horn at him from behind, nonstop, and driven him crazy. He had pulled out a metal club from who knows where and smashed up the Audi's hood and the windshield.

I had been close to flipping out like this on more than one occasion, maybe not as intensely as him, but enough that someone might have gotten hurt. I felt like a steel cable stretched to breaking point and snapping, recoiling with the force of so much built-up tension as to release all my frustration at the world at once, with total disregard. The courier had ended up in jail because he couldn't pay the compensation, or maybe he didn't want to pay.

Another case of the barefooted being unafraid of the well-shod—what more do the poor really have to lose?

Despite my many careful efforts, a customer did eventually complain, even though it was them who had given the wrong address. She had moved to the Tongjing Park neighborhood but had entered LC International North. These two neighborhoods were only a mile apart. Nothing about the delivery struck me as strange in the moment.

I remember it was a young man who answered the door and, when I said the recipient's name, took the parcel without a word—not, "That isn't me," or even a thank you. But this wasn't unusual. Some of us just don't like to talk. I encountered many people like this every day. And I'm no detective either. I'm not the sort to become suspicious of others for no real reason.

More than anything, though, I was very, very busy. It was one of those days when to save time waiting for the elevator, I would prop its door open with any object I could lay my hands on. But this meant I had to be conscious of taking too long with customers, in case I held up people waiting for the elevator on other floors.

Still, the complaint arrived two days later. The depot deputy notified me via WeChat that the recipient had reported the parcel as missing, yet it was showing as signed for and received. This particular breach was known as a "false signature and receipt," which came with a fifty-yuan fine (though I could appeal). I immediately called the customer. I had just left the Jinchengfu neighborhood on my trike. It was drizzling, so I pulled over. I often made calls while driving to save time, but not when I was angry.

"You reported me? It was your mistake," I said into my cell.

"I never got the parcel," she said, sounding aggrieved. "Why did you change the status to signed for?"

"Someone took it at the address you gave. Was I supposed to check their ID or something?"

"Sorry, I couldn't find your phone number in the app. I had no way of contacting you, so I tried customer service. I didn't say I wanted to complain. But they just took over."

I didn't entirely disbelieve her. Customer service was known to steer customers toward submitting complaints during the low season, as a way of pressuring us to improve the quality of our service. Whereas, at the crucial peak times, they would do everything in their power to defend us and avoid risking the stability and efficiency of order fulfillment. The depot lead and deputy had warned us about this. But I doubted the woman had really admitted the truth behind the mix-up—that she had left the wrong address on the order—which was why customer service filed a report for her. She was probably worried they wouldn't help her if she admitted her mistake.

Plus, my phone number was definitely displayed among the order tracking information. She said she couldn't find it, but maybe she had just been afraid of contacting me directly. I could refuse to help her, whereas with customer service mediating, my hands were tied.

Of course, this is just a hunch. I was never going to push her on the issue. She *had* just apologized, which for me meant she wasn't too proud to show a little courtesy, just impatient. So, I went back to LC International North to pick up her wayward parcel. It was still sitting on the side in the living room. A different tenant from the one I had met handed it to me, then I took it to the Tongjing Park neighborhood, which I passed every day on the road to Flagship Kaixuan, a block away.

When I found her, she was on the verge of tears, apparently feeling terrible about the whole situation. She said she would pay me back the fifty yuan. I had told her on the phone what her complaint would cost me. But I could have it annulled through appeal, if she explained to customer service that the situation had been resolved, so I turned down her offer. What I'd actually lost was three journeys' worth of time and money: dropping the parcel at the wrong address, going to collect it, and taking it to the correct address—all for her one parcel. The money didn't bother me so much. It was the wrongful accusation and the unnecessary extra hassle I felt angry about. There was probably also an element of discontent to my indignation: my unfair and unfriendly treatment, and all the unhelpful and inhumane rules and conditions I had to tolerate. But I couldn't unleash my anger on her, that would have meant I was just as bad.

I mentioned previously that there were two names in my "revenge list." Here, I'll tell the second person's story.

It was June or July and I was delivering a box of fresh fruit to an apartment in Sunshine New Town. When I arrived at the customer's door at eight-something A.M., I knocked, and no one answered. Cooled parcels demanded a different approach from regular ones, especially in summer, because if they weren't delivered quickly the food inside might turn.

Three calls to the customer's phone brought no answer. Normal procedure, if nobody was in and they weren't picking up, was that I should take the parcel away and try again in the afternoon. But the weather was blisteringly hot that time of year, and the storage in my trike felt like an oven from baking in the sun all day long. If I waited until the afternoon to come back, the fruit would already have gone bad. Maybe the customer would be back shortly, though; they might have only stepped out for breakfast or to pick up some groceries, in which case I could leave the parcel, and they would have it sooner rather than later.

I decided to leave the parcel in the neighborhood lockers. These lockers were between buildings number thirty-one and thirty-two, whose shade kept them out of the sun for most of the day. The customer's apartment was only a hundred meters away in building thirty-four. Since she hadn't answered my calls, I decided to send her a text message on top of the automated locker code she would receive, to tell her that this was a chilled parcel, and she should collect it as soon as possible.

Storing the parcel somewhere cool, in the shade, seemed at least better to me than keeping it in my trike. If she didn't come back beforehand, and didn't return my calls, then I would collect it myself on my second run of the neighborhood that afternoon. Any cooled parcels we hadn't managed to deliver had to be sent back in the evening, since there was no fridge in the depot.

I left the neighborhood around nine o'clock and called her twice more after finishing my rounds in Sunwangchang, then Jade Orchid Bay, in case she hadn't seen the text. But again, she didn't answer.

Sometime past twelve o'clock, she finally called back. I had just reached Flagship Kaixuan, about two miles from Sunshine New Town. I was sure she was phoning to thank me.

"I bought durians," she said. "Why did you put them in a locker?" She must have meant peeled durian flesh because the cool box wasn't big enough to hold a whole fruit.

"Nobody answered the door this morning," I reminded her.

"That doesn't mean you have permission to put my things in a locker. Bring it up to me, now."

I couldn't believe how harsh her tone sounded. I explained to her why I left the parcel there, then said, "I'm not in Sunshine New Town anymore. If it's convenient for you, you can go to collect it yourself. If you wait for me to come back, it will be another two hours."

"I can't wait," she said, "I have to leave. Come now and bring it to me."

I was already behind that day. I still had deliveries to make to two neighborhoods from my morning assignment, and it was hot. My mouth was dry, I was thirsty, and I didn't want to lose time bickering with her. "I can't now," I said. "If you can wait, I'll be back in Sunshine New Town in two hours. If you can't, then go get it yourself."

That was all it took for her to start threatening me. "I'm reporting you now. You never asked permission to put my parcel in the locker."

I didn't want to waste my breath. I hung up. Little did I think she would call again right away. I contemplated my phone for a moment and decided to answer.

"Are you bringing it here or not?" she asked. Of course, her tone wasn't polite. I explained where I was right then, but I could tell she didn't care one bit how far away I might be.

"It doesn't matter anyway. I can't come to you right now," I said. "Wait for me to get back to your neighborhood later, and I can drop it off. If you can wait, then wait."

"Why did you put it in the locker in the first place? Did I agree to that?" she went on.

"If I hadn't put your durian in the lockers, then it would be outside in the sun with me, cooking away until half past two. If you don't want to collect it, fine, I'll be in your neighborhood this afternoon and can deliver it then. But I'm not going now. I'm not your personal courier, I have many other neighborhoods to deliver to."

"You didn't even come to my door this morning!" she said.

This really pissed me off. "I called you three times from right outside your door. Why didn't you pick up?" I asked.

She didn't answer, but kept on repeating, "You can't put durian in a locker."

"Okay. Don't go get it yourself then. Wait for me," I said, hanging up. If she tried calling again, this time I wouldn't accept. She didn't. My hands were shaking with anger. She had bulldozed right over my good intentions. However, I still had parcels to deliver. I didn't want to throw away any more time on her.

She went to collect the parcel herself in the end, then reported me. But the complaint was thrown out when I appealed. I had saved my call log and text history from that morning, and the messages clearly showed that she hadn't been in. About half a month later, another box of chilled fruit came through, in a white polystyrene cool box like last time, though I couldn't say if it was durian inside or not. I went to her address in the morning and, sure enough, nobody was in, which suited me. I had called her before from the Tianjin Telecom number my company had given me, but this time I used my personal Yunnan Unicom sim. I was hoping she would reject an unknown caller from another province, that way I could take the parcel with me and leave it on the trike roof all day under the sun before going back to deliver it in the afternoon. But she answered straight away. I couldn't tell if she recognized my voice or not. "Should I deliver the parcel this afternoon?" I asked. I hoped she'd say yes.

But after a moment's hesitation she said, "Can you leave it in the lockers for me, please?" That was the last parcel I ever delivered of hers.

Compensation

Be a courier long enough and at some point, you will have to pay compensation. It was a bit of an inside joke among us: The more you work, the more you pay. The less you do, the less you lose. So, do nothing, lose nothing. There was one young guy at our depot who seemed to always get this wrong—he was paying damages for something new almost every other day. He soon quit for another industry.

There were more reasons than you could possibly keep tabs on why a courier might have to foot a bill. That young guy, for instance, was cursed with too much enterprising spirit for so green a worker, and it made him reckless. In an effort to boost his earnings, he took on a large area for his rounds. In the low season, this was a sound plan. But the moment things became busy, he struggled to keep up. That, combined with the capriciousness of young men like him, was a recipe for all kinds of problems. He received the most complaints of everyone, since he resorted to simply leaving parcels in neighborhood lockers without contacting customers first; he would never have been able to finish his work otherwise. But because Pinjun was the dedicated courier for the e-commerce website Vipshop, bad customer service like this wouldn't fly. The depot lead and deputy tried to defend him for a while, coming up with reasons to help with his appeals, but after repeated violations, they lost patience with him. Still, he never felt like he made enough and refused to give up any of his territory even though it was too much to manage.

He also lost a battery once. Trying to save time on a delivery, he parked his trike somewhere it wasn't secure, and when he returned only two minutes later, so he claimed, the battery was gone.

Parcels often went missing on his watch, too. He put a bagged package on the roof of his trike once, where normally it was only safe to leave the largest or heaviest items—he was probably trying to make his life easier by putting the parcels he was going to deliver first in the most accessible spot—but he hadn't ridden far out of the depot when the wind blew the parcel away. A sanitation worker reported that it was then taken by an elderly passerby. Inside was women's underwear, which might have only weighed a few dozen grams, but it cost more than four hundred yuan.

The courier was asking for trouble, basically. Increasing his income was all well and good, but with the amount of compensation he then had to pay, he can't have been earning all that much more than anyone else. He was also working himself to the point of exhaustion, which affected his mood. Plus, he ended up having to pay for a number of returns he collected for Vipshop because the products he brought back didn't match the orders. Though, to be fair, this happened to all of us.

Vipshop's returns process was different from Taobao and Tmall's: We weren't only responsible for collecting the parcels, we also had to check them ourselves. Customers would hand us the order for return, and we would select "Collection Successful" in the system, triggering an instant refund. We then sent the parcel back to the warehouse, where if the workers discovered any of the contents didn't match what the customer had requested to return, or there was any evidence of use that might affect resale, then the cost of the items would be deducted from our salary for that month.

Returns were a risky business for us and also ate into our day. A single order might include numerous items of clothing, up to twenty even, and we had to check each one in turn, then repackage and wrap them well before sticking on the return label. This took way longer than simply delivering a parcel, especially if the clothes were of an awkward design. There were also times a hole or lipstick stain would get past us, or we weren't careful enough handling white clothes with our always-dirty hands. Whatever the case, we had to pay.

The more common situation, though, was that the item a customer handed us didn't match the one on the order form. This could be because the customer had selected the wrong item when completing the returns form online, or because Vipshop had sent the wrong product to the customer in the first place. But if we failed to notice, then it was us who had to shell out.

I didn't pay a single fine as a result of a complaint the whole time I was at Pinjun, not that this is anything to brag about. But I had to pay compensation on three occasions. Two were because I didn't check carefully enough when collecting items for return, and they turned out to be different from what was stated on the order forms. In one of those cases, it was a light green children's outfit that I went to pick up, of which there were many different styles with various pictures on them, and it happened that the customer had received the wrong one in the first place. Vipshop had sent them a different design. But I didn't open the bag to properly check when I took the item from them. I just scanned the barcode on the bag, and that was correct.

Normally, this happened when another customer had previously returned an item of clothing in the wrong bag, so the barcode and product didn't match up. The warehouse worker who then dispatched the item when someone else bought it will have only scanned the packaging, rather than opening it to check, which was fine according to company policy. Only, when the second customer chose to return it because the design was wrong, the item will have remained in the system as the one the customer had wanted.

When the warehouse discovered the mix-up when placing the product back into inventory, I was ultimately the one held responsible since I'd missed that there was a mistake on collection. The whole thing was a little like the game "drum and flower," in which a flower is passed around players until the drumbeat stops, then whoever is holding the flower must do a forfeit, like answer a question, perform a song, or tell a joke. Whoever was the last to err in a series of errors was the one who paid the price. Fortunately, in this case, that price was only twenty-nine yuan, about the same as it cost to patch up a tire, so it didn't weigh on me too badly.

The other time was also on account of Vipshop dispatching the wrong item—a pair of Boerdiqi chunky sneakers, in the right style, with the right barcode on the box, but the pattern on the side of the shoes was slightly off. The brand had a whole range of chunky sneakers that looked almost identical and were easy to confuse if you weren't paying close attention. I must have been in a hurry that day and overlooked some detailing in the pattern. The sneakers cost 199 yuan, which I paid, and the warehouse sent me the shoes as if I'd bought them. I immediately posted them on Goofish, and they sold a few days later for 120 yuan. All in all, I only lost 79 yuan.

The third time I paid compensation was my most painful experience as a courier. Neither of those previous mistakes had set me back more than a hundred yuan, and frankly I was numb to small numbers like that by then. But the third instance cost me a thousand yuan and etched itself deep in my memory.

Having finished my deliveries in Jade Orchid Bay that day, I walked out of the neighborhood complex to find that a box of books from Dangdang that I had put on the trike roof was nowhere to be seen. My trike was parked in a row of delivery vehicles on the sidewalk, in the same spot I parked every day; you could even say it was my dedicated spot—although, only other couriers would recognize this. I had been delivering to Jade Orchid Bay for a year at that point and left parcels on the trike roof on most days it didn't rain. Not the mini-mountains of them that JD.com and TMall drivers piled on top of their trikes, but not a negligible number either.

Anyway, I had never heard of people stealing parcels from roofs before. Mostly what we left up there were unwieldy items that wouldn't fit inside, like bags of dog food or crates of beer or similar. Filching bulk packages like that could only have been hard work and was likely to attract a fair amount of attention. Plus, they weren't exactly valuable items in the first place, at least not to anyone other than the recipients. Like this box of books that went missing. I'm pretty confident that whoever stole it wasn't going to read them. Thirty or so pounds of books could have gotten someone twenty yuan if they were sold as scrap paper.

Of course, the thief might not have heard of Dangdang before, in which case they wouldn't have known what was inside the box. But even if they thought it was a crate of oil, or rice, or apples, or washing detergent, the effort and risk involved in stealing it would have far outweighed the returns—and this is saying nothing of the damage such behavior causes to one's character. Part of me even suspected the person didn't act out of greed but rather pure desire to harm me, just like some people will wantonly damage public property or abuse animals.

I immediately went to ask the other couriers and the security guards and sanitation workers in the neighborhood if they had seen anything, but nobody had. Some of them didn't even believe I'd lost the parcel, suggesting I'd simply forgotten it at the depot. Once I had eliminated every other possibility, confirming the parcel had been stolen, I felt all my will to finish the day's work drain from me. It was like I'd been flattened by a train, and I couldn't find it in myself to get back up. I have no memory of what happened next, or what I did for the rest of the day. For all I can remember I stood glued to the spot, in a daze, but I must have gone to the next neighborhood at some point, then the next one, going through the motions, until I finished my deliveries.

Back at the depot, the deputy helped me check the value of the parcel: one thousand–odd yuan. "I had a battery of mine stolen when I first started here," he said, trying to reassure me. "That was also over a thousand that I had to pay." But how this was reassurance I have no idea.

I took his advice, regardless, to file a report at the Jiukeshu public security bureau, though I wasn't hopeful they would be able to track the parcel down.

I was welcomed by a fat young officer with the accent of a true Beijinger. He had a great attitude even if he was too talkative. After making a written record, I asked him, "Do you think you'll catch the thief?"

"No one can guarantee that," he said. "I won't say for sure that we'll crack the case, but I can't say it's impossible either. Or else what are we for?"

"Can you show me the CCTV footage, please?"

"Unfortunately not. We have rules about that. I'll check it myself and get back to you." But I knew a colleague back at S Company who filed a police report and had been allowed to look at the CCTV with the officer. I mentioned this but was told it was about the timing. This was at the end of September 2019, and Beijing was in the middle of planning the seventieth anniversary celebration for the founding of the People's Republic of China. "This is an exceptional time. Higher-ups are keeping a close eye on everything, we don't want to overstep anywhere," the officer explained.

Shortly after I left, he called my cell phone. He must have been watching the CCTV footage while we were talking on the phone. He asked me for the precise location where I left my trike, and I described it in detail. "This camera is a little far from your trike," he said. "There are a lot of trees in the way. I'll think of something else." But I assume he never came up with anything, because I didn't hear from him again after that.

The box of books had been ordered by the T. T. Kindergarten next to Jade Orchid Bay. After confirming we couldn't retrieve the parcel, I went to discuss the question of compensation with the school. The parcel had been addressed to a middle-aged teacher there. She explained that the school was part of a chain, and it was the headquarters that had placed the order, so she wasn't clear herself which books had been inside or how much they were worth. She contemplated for a moment longer, then said that she seemed to remember receiving a list sent from HQ. After I added her WeChat, she sent me an Excel spreadsheet, with the inventory of the order. I asked how she wanted me to pay. "I can't take your money," she answered. "How about you help me to buy the books back?"

After getting home, I downloaded the Dangdang app and searched for each of the items on the list. They were all children's books, but none of them were cheap. However, I found some on Taobao at big discounts, and between the two sites I managed to buy the whole lot for only nine hundred or so yuan, so about one hundred less than the kindergarten originally spent. This was a small comfort.

We didn't know at the time that Pinjun Express would cease business operations in December of that year. Over forty thousand couriers across the country were laid off at once. The company sat on the announcement until the very last minute, perhaps for fear it would impact our morale. But after National Day, we all heard from S Company couriers that Vipshop had started trialing S Company as its new partner with a partial assignment of orders. Meanwhile, our daily workload had reduced. Looking back, there were lots of obvious signs—even at the end of 2018 when I had just started working there. As early as that, Vipshop had decided to let go of Pinjun Express.

Redundancy

For the eve of the Spring Festival, I had eaten my New Year's dinner together with the twenty-plus other couriers from the three depots managed by M at a small place in Xishangyuan. Compared with the banquet I'd had at S Company, it was a bit of a crummy affair. The dishes were fairly standard and didn't taste all that special, and the restaurant, which was hidden down a *hutong* rather than on a main street, clearly wasn't doing so well. We were the only two tables of customers there that evening.

But, I had just joined Pinjun and was feeling optimistic about the new work situation. I also got along well with my colleagues. So really, it didn't matter so much what we ate.

Halfway through the dinner, one of the regional managers named X appeared—he was M's supervisor. In a setting like that, it's not unusual for management to attempt an inspiring speech of some sort to encourage everyone. X did just that, adopting a very rousing tone, but the content of what he said was disappointing. He explained that after the Spring Festival, Vipshop's orders would no longer be handled exclusively by Pinjun, as some third-party merchants would now process and dispatch their own orders themselves. Returns and collections, though, would remain our responsibility.

I hadn't known how significant this was at the time. It was the initial step in Vipshop's transition away from using Pinjun's couriers: first, gradually hand over responsibility for third-party orders to merchants themselves, using this to trial for potential problems and make necessary adjustments, then give all Vipshop orders to S Company to deliver.

X went on, "In the New Year, the handling fee for Vipshop orders will reduce by two *jiao*." That's two tenths of a yuan.

"So, we'll have to collect more parcels if we want to earn more. Isn't that right, everyone?"

When a superior asks this sort of question to a group of employees, of course everybody is going to concur. Not to mention we already had our glasses raised. But X's logic, even a fool could tell it was wrong. He might have looked as delighted as if he was sharing the best of news with us, but we proletariat will never be anything but cynical of capitalist schemes. We had no illusions. Around June or July that year, the company lowered the handling fee by another 0.2 yuan. This time, no one warned us.

Yet, business for Vipshop was flourishing in 2019. The company had invested in an enormous promotional push, with product placements in several trending web series. This made it so that, in at least the first half of the year, the number of parcels we were handling didn't dip below the previous year's, even though we had lost a portion of third-party merchant orders. It might even have improved. This was the reason none of us expected that Pinjun Express would be dissolved come December. The company was developing at such a rapid pace, it seemed impossible that Vipshop would ever drop Pinjun.

But by October, S Company had started to take on Vipshop's self-processed orders, and the situation shifted. Our workload rapidly decreased. Still, S Company didn't nab all of the business at once. Vipshop integrated a monthlong buffer period into the transition, as more and more of the orders were given to S Company. There was no denying what was happening at this point, but Pinjun still didn't acknowledge it, continuing to send text messages that urged us not to believe the rumors and trying generally to make out like everything was okay.

Mostly, my colleagues remained unfazed and grounded throughout the process. Courier and food-delivery jobs were easy to come by in Beijing. If this company fired us, there was always a place for us elsewhere. As long as you were willing to work, you weren't going to starve. I also wasn't as trepidatious as when I first arrived at the start of 2018.

We joked that we had become "motherless children," as S Company gobbled up Vipshop's orders morsel by morsel, and large clients like Dangdang ceased to cooperate with Pinjun. As company operations ground to a halt, our workload shrank daily, and soon I could clock off at three, sometimes even two, in the afternoon. For Singles' Day we were only busy for all of five days maximum.

It is harder to find a new job at the end of the year, but nobody seemed to be in a rush. They would start thinking about what was next once it was 2020, they said. There seemed to be a shared sense that we were finally free, although we all knew this was only temporary. Nobody could have foreseen everything was going to become harder, in the new year, when the Covid-19 pandemic hit. But for the time being, what we cared about most was not the job search, but the size of the redundancy package we were going to receive. The daily discussions were lively, with everyone seeming to be full of curiosity and hope for the future.

Then, at last, the company announced that the payoff plan was "N+1." I had been at the company for fourteen months, so I would receive an amount equivalent to two and a half months' pay. The alternative option was a transfer to the nearby S Company depot, by way of the new working partnership between my old employer and Vipshop. This offer was on the table for all laid-off workers and included protection for our accumulated seniority and the continued provision of full insurance coverage. But there would be no compensation. I had already left S Company once, and knew very well that it wasn't for me, so I wasn't going back. Several of my colleagues didn't intend on moving, either. "We should be able go to S Company and also get the compensation," they said. Really, they never gave S Company a moment's consideration.

Our last shift at the company was November 25, 2019. I remember that each of us only had one or two parcels to deliver that day. After we were done, we went back to the depot to take down the freestanding shelves and wrap any of the stuff that the company wanted to save. Then we completed our employee resignation forms according to the deputy's instructions.

The deputy said there would be a recruiter from S Company coming in shortly to talk with us. We were experienced couriers with good knowledge of the local area, which made us significantly more reliable hires in the eyes of S Company than the average person off the street. But we weren't interested in S Company. Especially not me. I worried that the somebody coming to meet us would be Director L, given he was in charge of operations in Liyuan. His office was less than a mile away from our depot. Whatever happened, I did not want to see him, not then, not there, and not under those circumstances. So, we all headed out before he arrived, leaving only the deputy behind. "What do I tell the S Company representative when they get here?" he asked, helplessly.

Those final days with Pinjun were very relaxed. The pressure from work seemed to have completely evaporated, and I no longer felt anxious on my rounds. We even had time to chat for a while, after loading up the trikes in the mornings, before setting out. For over a year, I had been following the same established route every day to deliver the parcels—starting at Sunshine New Town, and going to Sunwangchang, Jinchengfu, Jade Orchid Bay, Jingtong Roosevelt Plaza, Jincheng Center, Carrefour, LC International Center, LC International North, LC International South, Hongxiang 1979 Cultural and Creative

Park, Donglang Film Industry Park, then Flagship Kaixuan, and finishing at Haitong Wutong Park. This seemed like the most sensible and efficient order to me, so much so that there were times I went off script and couldn't even complete that day's work.

But now I could experiment with doing the order in reverse, taking longer breaks whenever I could, even skipping over the middle places—though I'd always go back later once the industrial parks finally opened. I suddenly had plenty of time on my hands, like a once-scorned pauper who had struck it rich overnight. I got to enjoy the luxury of squandering time, as if it was a form of revenge. I had felt crushed by the constant need to exploit every second for so long, my time as tightly strung as my nerves, that I'd become used to work being just about coping. But now I was seeing Haitong Wutong Park and Flagship Kaixuan at eight in the morning for the first time, when I had worked in these places for over a year. With me arriving at each spot at "unconventional" hours, the sights and sounds I came across, and my feelings about the places, changed. I was seeing the work with new eyes. This wasn't just about the changes in habit, time, and place. I think it was more being able to approach it with a perspective not permitted to me until then because of the anxiety and stress created by the job—a perspective that was free from direction and purpose. I no longer thought of myself as a parcel-delivery robot that works for thirty yuan an hour and becomes angry and defeated at the first sign I might not meet my delivery quota.

Flagship Kaixuan was one of the neighborhoods I had always liked. It was a little rundown, but it was spacious and, with fewer residents than elsewhere, quite peaceful. Most importantly, trikes could be driven into the complex, which immediately meant that it was courier friendly.

One day, I put an apartment number into the call panel by a unit entrance there. It's not hard to imagine the sharp ringing sound that was about to start up in the apartment not far beyond the metal door, and the video intercom in that same apartment lighting up with my head or upper half appearing on the screen—depending how close I stood—staring awkwardly into the camera and struggling to disguise my impatience as I waited for the resident to answer.

Typically, none of this made for an exciting event, especially not for myself and the resident, who were total strangers. They might have been focused on some tasks for which quiet was essential, or they were a night worker recently back from their shift, or they were already sound asleep in bed when along I came and rang the doorbell, unceremoniously interrupting their day. So, over to the screen they stomped, frowning, to see who was being a nuisance. No wonder most residents seemed to growl when they spoke into the intercom.

Apartment 101 was the door I rang. The unit had six stories, with two apartments on each floor. Apartment 101 was on the left, a few steps inside the main door, and 102 was on the right, past the stairway.

I heard the urgent sound of the bell both through the intercom and from the apartment, before a man's voice asked who it was. Although there were two doors separating us, he was only a few meters from me.

After I replied, he started trying the door. There was a button on his intercom that must have been mechanical, because I could hear a loud click when he pressed it. I made deliveries in this neighborhood every day and knew there existed connection problems with some of the door-opening systems. Often, the buttons needed multiple presses before the door opened. This seemed to have annoyed some residents enough that they preferred to come straight out and let me in themselves.

But this resident was one determined individual, clearly someone who didn't easily compromise on their principles. Knowing full well that the button sometimes worked and sometimes didn't, he didn't place his hopes on anything happening on the first try. He rapidly jabbed the button repeatedly, causing the intercom to produce a long trilling sound like a flock of ducklings flapping their wings as they landed on water.

Meanwhile, I could only beam my most winning and encouraging smile at the camera, as thanks for him trying so hard. That way, this invisible drummer going wild backstage could see on the screen that his efforts were not going unappreciated, that I'd been swept up in his performance and was ready for the big ending—the door opening.

Though, as the sole audience member, I soon felt an awkwardness creep across my stiff features. Time was ticking, and I couldn't keep up the same generous, grateful smile. Yet, to drop it now would have been worse than never having smiled at all.

If I were to use a stock phrase to describe what I felt in that moment, it would be that time stopped. Seconds felt like years. Thirty passed, then sixty—was this ever going to end? I could lean into my role, but by then it would be time to snap out of it. Part of me even started to suspect the owner was playing games on purpose, and never intended to open the door. He might even have rehearsed this performance, all in order to teach me a lesson without the need for a showdown.

There was another version of myself inside me, an undoubtedly more honest and fearless version, who was already on the verge of yelling: It won't take you ten seconds to come and open the door, you moron! How much longer must you press the button?

It's a relief there still exist certain values in this world that transcend the utilitarian rules of gain and loss we've long placed our faith in. There are people who, for reasons inexplicable even to themselves, choose to live according to principles incomprehensible to others, and yet manage to carve out their own safe little corner all the same. It gives you hope that this world really could change for the better.

Motivated by some vague notion of universal love, I waited until the door finally opened. I stepped inside, and the resident was already standing in his doorway. He was a man of fortyish—an able-bodied man, might I add. I handed over his delivery, which he took, thanking me.

"My pleasure," I replied, politely.

Now that my days were so much easier and more enjoyable, I started trying to build better relationships with my customers. It would be my last chance before I had to say goodbye. There were some I felt I already shared a bond with, even if we knew too little about each other to be called friends. But ours were more than just business relationships; I felt like I had participated in and witnessed major parts of their lives: where they lived, their families, their pets, their different personalities and how they greeted others, the content of their baskets on Vipshop. I tried speaking to them with a playful attitude—in good faith, of course—and an overly humble tone. When they weren't in, I asked them what time they'd be home, and if I couldn't wait, I told them, "No problem, I'll drop it off when I come by after work." But their place wasn't on my way at all; I didn't pass any of these neighborhoods on my commute. I would make an extra trip because I was in a good mood, I had the time and, also, I was curious: Would they be flattered if I went out of my way to fulfill their requests, sparing no effort?

What I learned was that so long as I didn't care about being efficient, if I forgot about my return on investment, then every customer was easy to get along with, and they all gave me genuine smiles. Which shows that if there were no benefits or gains to be had, or losses to be made, this world really could be a harmonious and friendly place. And I'd still have time for myself. Which I did, time I spent reading after work again.

I read Robert Musil's *The Man Without Qualities*, which took me almost a month. I read very slowly, sometimes losing focus and having to go back and repeat sections. Then I revisited James Joyce's *Ulysses*. Both were books I had picked up before but never managed to finish.

It had been years since I had last read properly. It wasn't that I didn't read, it was that I couldn't manage to without significant effort. Work had long meant that I couldn't take in the words or information, which made me not want to sit down with a book at all.

In my last weeks with Pinjun, I often sat in Jingtong Roosevelt Plaza after finishing my deliveries and watched the passersby and the salespeople in stores, and the different delivery drivers riding back and forth. I observed their behavior, imagined their thoughts. Mostly I supposed they were numb, thinking nothing at all, feeling nothing, mechanically going about their days like I once had.

I also observed that, since I'd learned I was very soon going to leave this job behind, the majority of my thoughts were positive and beautiful. I had become a better person than I had been—at least, better than who I was at work—a kinder, simpler, more patient person. This told me that I hated this job, even hated all my jobs. Forced to go to work, I became irritable, grumpy, resentful, and I unfairly saw the customers I served every day as more selfish, unreasonable, and greedy than they really were.

Of course, I wasn't always a terrible courier. In fact, besides neither liking nor being good at communicating with clients, I was maybe the best of our depot in all other areas—of everyone, I came across as the most hardworking and responsible. But this wasn't to do with ability. Mostly it was because I never took on more than I could manage—others overloaded themselves with work to make more money, but what they received were frequent complaints. As a result, I didn't earn a lot. I wasn't even in the top handful of earners in the depot. But which customer thinks about how much a courier earns when they're choosing between giving five or three stars?

Before I left the job, I posted on my WeChat Moments so only customers could see, informing them about Pinjun Express's dissolution, and that I wouldn't be taking on Vipshop deliveries in the future. Lots of customers commented, praising my attitude, and thanking me for my longstanding service. It improved my assessment of my work, slightly—I was under the impression I'd done abysmally. One customer wrote, "You're the hardest working and most responsible courier I've seen." I don't have a very strong memory of her if I'm being honest, so it was a surprise that she would rate me so highly. But I trust that she was being sincere. There was no benefit to her giving me empty praise at this point, since our business together was over. We were very likely never going to meet again. So, I'd like to sum up my time as a courier as follows, and it's no exaggeration: I was once the best courier that some customers had ever seen.

3

Odd Jobs in Shanghai

The Convenience Store

When I moved to Shanghai, I rented a room in a small partitioned apartment on the first floor of a residential building in a Qinzhou North Road neighborhood. The room was dark and dank, but I saved money by renting from the landlord directly, without an agency. There were two other occupied partitions in the apartment, a communal toilet, and a living area. There was no kitchen. My room was the smallest, and my rent the lowest. The five or so usable square meters included a bed, a wardrobe, and a desk. That was all. To use the desk, I just sat on the bed's edge. The rent was 1,500 yuan.

I had found my job on 58.com. The site wasn't nearly as much of a hub for fraudsters as it is today, and finding work there was easy, especially if it didn't require a diploma. Generally, I only tried companies that I had heard of, like D and S Companies when I later became a courier. Well-known enterprises aren't free of problems, of course, but there was still a lower likelihood of stepping on a landmine with them. In the end I went with C Conveniences.

Before starting, I had to complete a company training in a high-tech industrial park in the north of the city. C Conveniences' headquarters was tucked away in a low office building. There were a dozen-plus of us who attended and took the practical test: The chief examiner read off a list of products, which we put through an imitation cash register; the shopping lists covered all the usual daily tasks and register operations we would have to carry out in the store. If we calculated the total bill correctly, we passed. The exam wasn't very difficult, but several people were still asked to come back for another round of training, or they were welcome to look for a job elsewhere.

Based on my address, the company assigned me to a nearby branch in Xuhui District. The shop manager was a woman in her thirties, from Jiangxi. When I turned up to report, she introduced herself and showed me around the store. There were four employees there at the time, all women. They had put in a request that the company hire a man—that was me—to take the long night shifts. She wanted to gauge how I felt about this. I could always refuse. But I liked working at night. It meant dealing with fewer customers.

My main tasks would include processing a delivery of goods in the very early morning, then cleaning around the store. The deli counter, in particular, took some work to get spotless. Once that was done, I had to prepare the snacks that would be kept warm there—the *oden*, mini hotpots, steamed dumplings, and whatnot—as well as the drinks, like the soy milks and coffee.

I didn't find out my salary until after I started. The HR department had previously explained the salary structure, but a part of it was dependent on the store's business, which I had no way of predicting. Colleagues eventually told me that, after deducting social insurance, they ended the month with a little over three thousand yuan in their pockets. For doing night shifts, I would receive a modest bonus of four hundred yuan extra.

Even so, all I had left after rent was about two thousand yuan to get me through the month, which wasn't much considering I had no kitchen and had to eat takeout for every meal, spending around thirty yuan a day. Then there were the usual living costs. This might have been why the manager said we could eat any of the deli meals on the shelves that had passed the sell-by date. This was actually against the rules, as all out-of-date food had to be discarded, a task the manager had to sign off on. But if the manager had done as she was told, she would have been the only person working there—it just wouldn't have been worth it for the lower-paid employees. These free meals were her way of helping us to reduce expenses and keeping staff around. The rice balls, sushi, cold noodles, and other chilled savory goods were also free to take as soon as they passed their shelf life. One day the manager even gave me an out-of-date two-pint carton of milk.

I arrived at the store in the evening every day and left the next morning. The company stipulated that we work sixty hours a week. But the manager told me that if we stuck to the sixty hours, the store would need to hire another employee and everyone's individual income would dip below three thousand yuan, so she scheduled everyone to do something like seventy-two hours per week. Working more to earn more. I didn't have a problem with that, I told her. Though I couldn't have said no, in reality. This was a group decision.

The convenience store wasn't hard work, but it was boring. There was just so little to do at night. I resorted to scrubbing the oily deli counter very slowly, and repeatedly polishing the large tempered-glass door with newspaper and glass spray. Occasionally, the waiters from Spicy House, the Sichuanese place next door, would come in for a chat mid-shift. But I didn't know them all that well, and I'm not great at small talk.

In the end, I worked at this C Conveniences for fewer than ten days.

It was one morning, at some time past six o'clock, when I was in the store on my own waiting for my colleague to take over the early shift, that a middle-aged woman came in and bought a cup of soy milk. She would become my next boss, Y.

Y had opened a bike shop nearby. She hadn't really come for the soy milk, but to recruit me. Her last cashier had embezzled her money and run off, so now she was in a hurry to hire someone. She couldn't even wait to post a job listing. Instead, she had spent the morning going around the nearby convenience stores—the 7-Eleven, Lawson, and FamilyMart, and now us, all within two hundred meters of her shop—trying to recruit the cashiers.

Y could talk, so I quietly listened and let her speak. She told me that of the cashiers on shift I was the only one wearing a face mask. This was a requirement at all the companies, but it might not have been so strictly enforced on the night shift workers. She offered me a three-thousand-yuan base salary with the chance for commission, and I could stay in her shop—this is what really attracted me to the job, since I could save the fifteen hundred yuan I was dropping on rent every month. She also promised me full insurance coverage, then never honored her word, buying group health insurance instead. She later justified her decision by saying that social security is a con. As long as you had medical insurance you were okay. When I dropped a sofa on my face in the shop warehouse, six months later, trying to get it down from high up, it just missed my eye. I went to Ruijin Hospital for stitches and took full advantage of the group insurance payout.

Y was so desperate to hire that I didn't even have a chance to resign according to the proper protocol. The store manager initially insisted that I complete at least a month there, but she must have started to worry that my lack of commitment would cause problems, because two days later she approved my application for immediate resignation. A colleague then told me that I had been blacklisted by HR and wouldn't be allowed to work at C Conveniences again.

I had quit lots of jobs before, but this time weighed on my conscience the most. I felt like I owed the store manager. Since I was still working nearby afterward, I waited a few days, then bought some fruit to drop off there as an apology. But when I reached the entrance, I froze at the doorway, unable to build up the courage to enter. I paced back and forth for a quarter of an hour on the opposite sidewalk and eventually abandoned the idea. I ate all the fruit myself.

When I left the room on Qinzhou North Road, I lost both the rent for the remainder of that month and the deposit, as was stated would happen in the contract if I left before a month was up. That was two thousand yuan altogether. I arranged to meet the landlord to explain the situation and told him I would have hardly any money until my paycheck came through. My hope was he would take pity on me and show a little mercy. He handed over two hundred yuan without a word, and that was that.

The Bike Shop

I worked for a little over a year at Y's store, passing C Conveniences almost every day. I would walk by the entrance as quickly as I could, never daring to pause for even a moment. Sometimes my new colleagues would go in to buy things while I hid somewhere farther up the street. It made them laugh. When C Conveniences paid my wage for the measly few days I was employed there, part of me wanted to turn it down. But it shows there is a benefit to working for a well-known company: They tend to stick to the rules and treat people impartially.

Y's shop, meanwhile, had its issues. Staff morale was low. The situation, it turned out, was not as simple as one cashier having cut and run. The shop sold a high-end American brand of bicycle, for which there was a single chain store in the country, and thirty or so franchises. Of all the franchises, Y said that hers was the only one run by the owner themself. What she meant was the other franchise locations were started by enthusiasts out of a love of cycling and belief in the brand, rather than by businesspeople with profit in mind. After joining the franchise and opening their stores, the other owners would hire someone else to be the manager, whereas Y founded this one and also worked there.

She wasn't even a cyclist—at least, not back then. She hardly knew her way around a bike, though she would never have admitted as much. She was an enthusiast, not about bikes necessarily, but about ambition and the social fulfilment she derived from her work—she wasn't someone who enjoyed being on her own. If she had been selling furniture instead, I'm certain she would have appeared just as enthusiastic about tables and chairs.

The key was her sheer competence and energy. From what she had learned at the periodic company-wide training sessions alone, she was always able to find something to say about any part of a bike, even if it was all just hot air. So, when I say she didn't understand bikes, I mean relative to cyclists—to people who *loved* bikes. Next to anyone else, she was no doubt the expert. In a past life, she had been a marketer for a foreign company, and had all the makings of a "top seller": the extreme enthusiasm, positivity and optimism, the gumption and resilience. She was a go-getter, and she loved to chat. Every time a customer came in the door, I could almost hear the dopamine coursing through her body. To me, greeting customers was something I needed to mentally prepare for, but for her there was nothing more thrilling.

Yet, when it came to interacting with real cyclists, Y kept a reserved attitude, since they often knew more about bikes than she did and were harder for her to sway. They were also quite careful about what they bought. Often, they wouldn't make a purchase until they were absolutely sure they had what they needed. This was in part down to a sensitivity to price. Most of them liked to compare their options thoroughly before buying and were more likely to come into the store to look around than to spend their money. When they eventually did buy something, it was rarely in her shop. In her words, "Cyclists are all poor." So, she had different ideas about who we should be catering to.

"Property in this area costs upwards of ten thousand yuan per square foot," she liked to point out. "Our target market is whoever lives in those apartments." As far as she was concerned, it would be bad business to open a store in a goldmine like that and still be wasting energy thinking about cheapskate cyclists. So, she displayed several commuter bikes fitted with child seats outside the shop. Bikes for doing groceries or picking up a kid from school were not what serious cyclists were looking for, and the fact the brand released any at all hurt its image as a company targeting sophisticated sportspeople. But the small range was the brand's way of compromising with the market. Y simply saw the benefit of the compromise more than others. She even stretched to adulterating her stock with other brands' products, including folding bikes. In a roundabout way, it was fortunate that the brand's market size in China still hadn't caught up to what it was even in a country as small as New Zealand, and that most of the stores still hadn't made a profit, because the company spared her a hefty fine despite her violating the licensing contract, among many other transgressions.

Y's preferred customer was the slightly older, well-heeled type, one with buying power and a budding interest in cycling that hadn't yet progressed past the first big step. Faced with these sorts, she had a knack for turning their "I'm just looking, thanks" into cash or credit. Her strategy was to wear them down: Whatever reason a customer came up with to refuse, she could propose an alternative, even if sometimes her plans were a little forced. She also did more than just flap her lips. If the customer hadn't voiced a clear no about the bike she was trying to push on them, she would send one of us staff to fetch a boxed model from the underground stockroom in a residential complex next to the shop. We then assembled it in front of the customer and let them have a test ride—for some customers she did this with four, even five bikes to make a sale, delaying closing the store by an hour or two (We normally shut at 9 P.M.). Customers often softened at seeing all the trouble we were going to, and the sweat we shed, while Y stood at the side reeling off the bike's various specifications. The glimmer of curiosity or interest that had brought them in the door had stopped short at "wanting to find out more before they made a decision," but Y did everything in her power to help that happen before they left the same way. She didn't like when customers said they would be back later, not unless she had already received their deposit. She believed that most consumption is impulsive—if everybody insisted on having time to think, then nobody would ever buy anything.

In a nutshell, her work style balanced mine perfectly. I felt very little pressure when we were on shift together. Talking with customers was a nightmare scenario in my mind, and if she was there, I didn't need to. She took on all the parts of the work I didn't like. Meanwhile, she had me do any heavy lifting or organizing of the stockroom, which I was fine with. But the method to Y's madness ended there—and by madness, I mean her personal brand of chaos.

She would put things down and forget where she left them, and often tried to juggle so many tasks at once that she'd lose track of what she had said or done. She took a customer's deposit once without logging the purchase, because she was too busy, so all they had was a verbal agreement between them which, of course, slipped her mind the moment she started on something else. When the customer came back to collect the bike, she had no memory of them. A colleague and I had to find the customer's card info in the system by matching the amount to their account transactions.

But you wouldn't have known she was forgetful. She treated everybody like they were an old friend. Sometimes she couldn't recognize customers who knew her, yet she still gave them a warm and gushing greeting while managing not to get caught out.

Hers was an almost pathological anxiety, which would not let her stay calm and led to a lot of capriciousness. Like the time she labelled a bike with a special price only to peel it off hours afterward. "Why discount a bike when nobody's going to see it," she said, laughing at herself. I then watched her putting another sale sticker on the very same bike just hours later, because people were even less likely to see it if there was no label at all. Yet there'd been barely a handful of customers in all day. She went around and around like this constantly, fretting over every win and loss like an ant on a hot pan: If a move didn't yield instant results, then it was a wrong move. This didn't help her already terrible emotional regulation. She was notorious for it—she often blew up at us then apologized, only to do the same again a few days later. Erupt, then say sorry. It gave the impression her apologies meant nothing.

In all these ways, Y and I were opposites. I'm gentle, even-keeled, rarely excitable. I'm very methodical, I like to keep a workspace clean and can't function in messy surroundings. I was there to support Y, to tidy, and to reassure and remind her, and as a result she became more efficient.

But the rest of the staff, perhaps besides the part-timers, all hated how Y went about her work and relationships. Unlike me and her, they chose this industry because they loved cycling. Outside of work, they were the very cyclists that Y avoided. Nobody in the trade sold bikes like Y did, they said. It tired them out how busy they were under her—busy mostly with what they saw as pointless tasks. All of Y's cajoling of customers and making staff carry and assemble bike after bike irritated them. They called it a "confidence game," her pretending weakness as a way of winning the customer over: a hard sell made cheaply. She wasn't even the one who put in the heavy lifting, we were the ones left dripping with sweat. So, every customer who left without buying anything was further proof that they were right: Y's constant fussing had us running around like headless chickens for nothing.

She would sometimes treat us staff the way she treated customers, running her mouth at a million miles an hour, making all sorts of promises, only to regret them later. It was messy stuff. But Y wasn't afraid of mess, I don't think. She said she was, but her behavior and decisions told a different story, and the outcomes were almost always predictable. She had gone into an industry in which she had to rely on the expert technical knowledge of a small number of colleagues for her business to be successful, because while she was the boss, she was also essentially a salesperson—her perspective, her skill set, her personality were all tuned to a sales role. And the store was first and foremost a business, in her view, not a pastime. She wasn't wrong. But she depended on a select few people who were only there out of interest.

When I first started at the store, she had two full-time employees named J and S, who were technicians. While talking with them, it surprised me to discover that they both sympathized with and supported my predecessor, the cashier who embezzled store money. I had thought that corruption was a black-and-white question, but they thought Y had acted worse than the cashier. They were good to me, though, very friendly, and I was friendly with them. I didn't argue or compete, I didn't contradict anyone. I was the perfect gentleman. It later became clear that these two were the best of the employees that Y hired. Their replacements, when they each left, lacked their professionalism and expertise, as well as their moral fiber.

But Y still tried to sabotage my and J's relationship early on. She told me not to get too close to him because he would be leaving us very soon. J had been a technician at the brand's flagship store, so he was the best "official technician" we could have. The flagship store and headquarters were both in Pudong District. Shanghai was the only city in the country at the time that boasted two of the brand's stores. Y had poached J to be her store's manager with the lure of a high salary.

But the store didn't need another manager; it had Y, whose personality was much better suited to management than J's. He was amiable and easygoing, and maybe a little lax. But he was a very skilled technician and could also lead store events, like rides through the city or in the nearby hills. He had plenty of experience there. So he was essential to the store's survival. We couldn't rely on bike sales alone, even if the levels of consumption in Shanghai were quite high, since bikes that cost tens of thousands of yuan apiece were not going to fly off the shelves. Unlike with cell phones, people don't really change their bike setups on a yearly or two-yearly basis. So consumable goods, equipment, experience, and customer service were much bigger draws for customers. A weekly event or two was therefore a must.

But according to Y, she paid J a store manager's rate, so he should assume a manager's level of responsibility. This was the root of their disagreement. When Y first took over the store, she was, on the one hand, very insecure since she didn't understand bikes or the industry. But at the same time, she was optimistic. She was confident that she knew how to run a business, while a lot of other bike shop managers, she discovered, didn't. They were all far too laid-back. She even told me, disdainfully, that compared with her previous employer, another foreign company, the administration at our brand HQ was amateurish, disorganized, and ineffective. I got the impression she thought that if our brand had been in a more ruthless industry, it would have long ago been driven into the ground by its competitors. Her taking on the bike trade was her own version of the "dimensionality reduction attack" from *The Three-Body Problem*. She was using her "three-dimensional" skill set to dominate what was, relatively speaking, a "two-dimensional" field.

This was why she offered J the "big bucks" to come work for her, to increase her chances of success. However, she hadn't accounted for personality and ideology being bigger determiners of effectiveness than ability. When it became clear that J wasn't going to meet her expectations, she went at him with everything, which only made him dislike her.

I didn't appreciate that Y wanted me to take sides, but I never told her this: I hate being dragged into others' arguments, it only hurts my happiness and quality of life. They can solve their own issues, was my stance. I'm staying neutral, and only neutral. What's more, J and S saw me as one of them, another worker, while Y was our boss and therefore set against us. I often went with S and some of the later hires for mini hotpot at a place at the Xiangyang and Yongjia intersection.

Like most bosses, Y wouldn't stand for her employees idling on the job. If there were no customers in the store, she could always find something for us to do, like cleaning or inventory. For historical reasons, our stock was incredibly chaotic, which wasn't helped by us moving stockroom twice in the time I was there. At one point, she decided she wanted the inventory checked weekly, but that never really happened.

This was the difference between a team led by a boss, and one led by a hired manager: When I was at C Conveniences, for example, we were allowed to sit back all we wanted if our duties were complete, and the manager wouldn't say a thing. In fact, she would be relaxing herself. But for Y, as the boss in charge, the mere sight of dawdling employees spelled loss, so she made sure to put us to work immediately.

As the new cashier, I was the one who noticed the point-of-sale system was outdated, and a lot of the data redundant. Of course, the person who knew how it had ended up like this was no longer at the company to point out what needed clearing. In fact, there were so few employees in the store that the daily divisions of labor readily blurred. Everybody worked the cash register now and again, and I often had to leave my post at the counter to retrieve stock or greet customers and assist them with test rides. So, we were all guilty of forgetting to log products as sold when it became busy. Some products, like helmets, only had a barcode on the box. If a customer tried on multiple different sizes or styles, whoever was assisting them might put the helmets back in the wrong boxes, which would lead to all sorts of confusion when we eventually did scan them out of the stockroom for a sale. We couldn't look to Y to lead by example here, either. She was the worst offender. She was extremely careless and had no mind for detail. Anyway, these are all the many reasons our cash register could only be used for printing receipts, and why the inventory data was so unreliable.

Our regular working hours were "996," which in ordinary language means we were open nine to nine, six days a week. But customers often lingered past nine. On the rare occasion that Y wasn't in, we would kindly ask that the more indecisive customers come back tomorrow. But with Y at the helm, if there was any customer in the store—even an old man shuffling around in sliders, with his hands clasped behind his back, who had dropped in on an evening stroll—we absolutely could not shut. There were times I couldn't tell whether Y loved this job or hated it. Some of her methods just seemed like ways of punishing herself and us in the process. I mean, which workers enjoy doing overtime? Let alone ones as relaxed and unambitious as J, S, and me. We didn't even like doing sales. Y was the store's number one seller, and with her managing to cope on her own, the rest of us weren't going to make any commission. So, from a financial perspective, extra work was time wasted for everyone.

This being our attitude, it made sense that she put so much emphasis on team building. In a store that was open every day and never much allowed us to hang out, this took the shape of many after-work meals. I ate plenty of seriously good food that year. A seafood buffet, for one. It was on the top floor of a fancy hotel, so elegant, and I walked up wearing a sweat-stained work T-shirt. High-end places like that used to make me feel self-conscious. I worried that I was going to make a fool of myself. Sometimes, just a look from a waiter could sting. So, I didn't really enjoy those perks to the full. Eventually, I started requesting Saizeriya every time Y asked where I wanted to eat. That's the Japanese chain that serves Italian. It could never match the seafood buffet, but at least I wasn't on edge eating there, peering over my shoulder all the time. I could let loose a little.

Y insisted that we use every moment to be productive, but she was also very happy to spend money on meals out in the hope we might all build better relationships. Most other bike-shop bosses didn't operate like this. Y had a tendency to be excessive: asking for too much while also giving too much; hurting us more than she should, and going overboard with her apologies . . . She struggled with calm. Her days were spent in a constant state of excitement—she was a born fighter.

There was also a number of part-timers at the store. One of them was a college student who I'll call L, who drove a BMW in to work. This didn't even mean he was second-generation rich, by Shanghai's standards, just that his family had healthy finances. He was an impressive guy, really. He had a firm expertise, knew how to communicate, and was good with his hands, and in his spare time he regularly placed well in road races and Ironman competitions. Y paid to send him to a bike-fitting course, and for a long time he was our shop's only fitting technician. L's customers spent a lot of money, so Y would send him some of the more knowledgeable or higher-budget clients, for him to push the most upscale models on. Being an athlete himself, L knew how the bikes performed and what their pros and cons were. Those customers trusted salespeople speaking from experience. Meanwhile, Y knew how to handle those newer to the sport.

Around about when J and then S left, there started a period of constant transition, with lots of new hires and quick departures. D and W were the most notable characters of the bunch.

D had previously been a pharmaceutical sales rep for a foreign company. He had left because he liked cycling and wanted to open his own store. Originally, Y promised that she would take him on as a partner in the future. But it wasn't long before she started to complain about his work ethic and went back on her word, as well as on several other promises.

D believed he had been scammed by Y. He was furious. After a big argument, he took the opportunity while Y was away for the Spring Festival to steal some bikes from the stockroom, with a total sales value of forty thousand yuan. Wilder than that was, after he'd stolen the bikes, he then came back to demand the commission that Y owed him. He knew Y had no evidence that he was the thief.

The shop was undergoing renovations that holiday period, and all the inventory had been packed into the stockroom. D must have had a duplicate key cut, because the door and lock were left intact. The bikes he stole had never been on display in the store, anyway—one was on layaway, and another had been put aside for a customer—so it was more than a month before we finally noticed they were missing. The CCTV outside the stockroom only stored the previous fourteen days of footage.

Despite the lack of evidence, everybody understood it had been D. He was always stealing things from the shop. He also knew the stockroom well and could sneak the bikes out undetected. With the store under renovation, the stockroom a mess, and Y not in Shanghai, he chose the perfect moment to strike. Only an employee could have had such insider perspective. Plus, the bikes we lost were ones he always talked about. Two of them were Colnago single-speed road bikes, which cost thirty thousand yuan alone. D was the only "single-speedster" in the store. He adored retro road bikes like those, while the rest of us weren't really interested in them. He collected them, just to collect, and the bikes he took weren't even the most expensive models in the stockroom.

This wasn't his first offence, either. He had previously pilfered various equipment and parts with the help of W. Sometimes they simply stole them. Other times they made out like the items were gifts for customers, only to keep them for themselves. D never even tried to conceal this fact from me early on, instead acting as if what he was doing was totally normal, as if there was no question I'd support him. I didn't tell anyone what I knew, but I also didn't facilitate him continuing: I just pretended I had no idea. Whenever he took anything, I would remind him to pay, and leave it at that. He eventually realized I didn't want to be involved and hid his actions from me from then on. Meanwhile, W was siphoning business from the store, pocketing the money from a number of regulars who came to him for repairs or bike services. This was straight embezzlement.

J and S knew full well what their two younger colleagues were up to. They didn't take part, but neither did they disapprove. Forgetting morals for a moment, D and W were both easy guys to get along with: W was very happy-go-lucky, and D likeable and witty. The four of them also spoke a common language in cycling and had plenty they could talk about. They were closer with each other than any of them were with Y, and the senior technicians sympathized with the boys enough not to give them up or stop them. It felt like a repeat of the situation with the runaway cashier.

D and I took a fundamentals course together in Shanghai Zhangjiang Hi-Tech Park, and also attended our company's annual general meeting in Xiamen. Y paid for us to do both. The time in Xiamen, we stayed at a nice hotel and ate really well. We also made a day trip to Gulangyu, the pedestrian-only island just off the coast of Xiamen, and of course stopped by Taiwan Snacks Street on the way to the ferry. We tried all sorts of enticing local specialties that tasted of the ocean. Sea worm jelly, oyster omelets, sweet peanut soup, fish balls with surprising fillings. The flavors were difficult to describe in a few words, but they were certainly unforgettable.

Friendship, though, wasn't the reason I kept quiet. That was job security, plain and simple. In the general makeup of the store, I was the mere flunky who disliked common enemy number one least of everyone. But I was earning more there than I had at C Conveniences, and the work was more interesting. I didn't want to have to give the job up just because I'd made myself into an outcast.

Putting aside D's flaws for a moment, I've always thought it sad that he was the only one in the store who ever showed Y's dog any love. Lucky was the dog's name (he doesn't need an alias). In 2013 he had just turned one year old, and was an overactive and mischievous little rabble-rouser. The other guys hit the puppy almost every day, sometimes so much that he lost control of his bladder all over the ground. Y had taken him in when she found him abandoned outside the store door, a newly born puppy. He was a mutt, with yellow-brown fur and white patches on his paws and belly, and a very long, thin muzzle and dropped ears, and the slender waist of a hunting dog. He was very quick, too quick to easily catch.

Something related to speed would have been a better name for him, really, since Lucky was a misnomer. He spent his days being terrorized by a group of tired and grumpy, sometimes vindictive, shop workers with a lot of feelings to get off their chests, and he *was* the boss's dog, which was an unforgivable sin to begin with. So, it's easy to imagine what happened when he started being a nuisance. But D never hit Lucky. He fed the dog daily and sometimes took it out for a walk without even being asked.

I didn't hit Lucky either, to be fair, but I wouldn't say that I liked him. At most, I posted on my WeChat Moments insinuating that I didn't agree with people hitting dogs. Y agreed to me finding adoptive parents for Lucky, but everyone I asked was unwilling to take him on. He wasn't purebred, and I didn't know enough people locally who were well-equipped to look after a dog.

Since I lived in the store, walking Lucky naturally became my responsibility. Every evening after we closed and everyone else had gone home, I would still have to do the day's accounts and take Lucky out. I'd watch him proudly piss everywhere and picked up his steaming turds with newspaper. I led an even lamer life than the dog. It was often past 11 P.M., and sometimes midnight, by the time I could finally settle down for the evening. I felt like I had zero time to myself or any freedom.

I lived in the store for six months before W moved in. I didn't like living with other people, so I found myself a place shortly after through an estate agent: a partitioned room on the upper floor of a building in the Yi Shiyijia neighborhood, on the south side of Shanghai Indoor Stadium. There were five rooms in the apartment with one person to each. We shared a living area and bathroom, with no kitchen. Rent was 1,800 yuan per month, which I could manage by then on my wage. My room was northeast facing. Outside the window was the Inner Ring Elevated Road, and across it the Shanghai Indoor Stadium.

I enjoyed going for runs around the stadium when I could. Ten kilometers was my usual distance, though I did run a half marathon once. I also liked to stroll around the Lianhua Supermarket there, and I would while away my days off in IKEA, because it was nearby and had AC. I'd find a couch and curl up for a nap, which nobody seemed to mind at first, but eventually the capitalists removed their mask of kindness and sent security to move along anyone who was sleeping—because you can't wake up someone only pretending to be asleep, the only ones disturbed were those of us genuinely there to get some rest.

I didn't buy furniture in the store, but I often took advantage of the Absolut Vodka promotion in the first-floor food shop. A bottle of vodka cost around one hundred yuan on discount and came with a free bottle of juice. I'd then spend the evening sitting by my window drinking and looking out at the bustling streets. I felt especially serene in those moments. Though this might have just been the alcohol.

When I lived in the bike shop, I had one day off per week, a weekday typically, and if I stayed in the store that day, then Y would be constantly badgering me, asking for help. So, I always went out. Suzhou, Hangzhou, Wuxi, Zhouzhuang, Wuzhen,

Xitang—I explored many of the places around Shanghai over that period, mostly on group tour buses, which left at 7 A.M. from the Shanghai Tourism Center to the south of the stadium. My fellow tourists were mainly elderly people. Tickets often cost less than a hundred yuan and included lunch, and though the tours always called in at various shopping areas along the way, the guides wouldn't hold it against you if you didn't buy anything. I'd still try to get some cheap local specialties to take home, though.

If I didn't go on a group tour, then I would jump on the subway and visit the various suburbs of Shanghai. For example, I passed a whole day sitting in Drunken Bai Garden and Fangta Park, in Songjiang, and also went to Thames New Town where there was a lake and a church, and all the architecture was in the style of British market towns. There were several newlyweds there having their photos taken. I also ate Nanxiang soup dumplings in a restaurant surrounded by greenery, over in Guyi Garden in Jiading, and of course saw Yu Garden, the Bund, Nanjing Road, and People's Square in the city center. I went to all these places on colleagues' recommendations. It was a precious thing to have somewhere I could spend a day making memories.

Fuxing Park was one of the places I returned to regularly. I could walk there from the store. A favorite spot of mine was the wooden benches next to the sunken flower beds, where I would sit and read and occasionally lie down for a snooze. I made sure to always have insect repellant with me, so I didn't have to leave before dark. It was there that I used to see foreign women, in hot pants and tube tops, sunbathing on the grass. I was astonished when I saw their model-like bodies and gorgeous faces, but I didn't stare at them or even peer their way when I passed by, out of dignity and respect. Mostly I was surprised that the elderly folk in the park acted like they were invisible. None of them even stopped to look or did a double take. Shanghai was already a very cosmopolitan place by then, and the locals were used to seeing the faces of the world. Yet the elderly at the open-air tearoom might have tutted if a young man like myself joined them for a pot of tea. I should have been out contributing to society rather than sitting on my rear end, slowly sipping my days away.

Now that I was selling bikes for a living, I was also riding them. Not in the mountain events, but I often joined the road ones. If it was a store activity, then I would use one of our brand's aluminum road bikes. On my own, I rode a very old custom bike. Y had assembled both these beginner setups for me. Otherwise, I tried my best to avoid models that I couldn't afford, since accidents were almost inevitable. When I first started wearing clip-in cycling shoes, I fell off once and scratched my face, and the cut became infected, which made my lip swell and left me looking like an alien for days.

When by myself, I mostly rode on Longteng Avenue, not too far from the store. Back then, what is now the south side of the Xuhui Binjiang Greenbelt was a popular meetup area for bikers in the evenings, with people on all different kinds of bicycles gathering there to kick back and make friends. Even motorcyclists would turn up with their great big engines. Shanghai definitely has the best bike culture and atmosphere, as well as the most bikers, of all the places I've lived, even better than Beijing and Guangzhou. It still has a long way to go to catch up with cities in Europe and America, though.

Y tried hard to talk me into buying a bike. She said she would sell me one at the purchase price, because I wouldn't survive long in the industry if I didn't have my own. But that was still at least a month of my salary, excluding upgrades and fitting costs. Dropping such a large sum of money in a single purchase was a terrifying prospect, so I never did in the end.

Before the Spring Festival, the real estate agent informed me the apartment I was in was being reclaimed by the bank. I had to find another place to stay right away. I moved to a neighborhood on Lingling Road, into a two-room apartment I would share with the real estate agent. He became my sublandlord. The rent was 2,300 yuan. Y offered to pay me an extra 500 yuan every month to cover the increase. Only, the landlord and I didn't get along. It's unusual to invite friends to stay overnight without checking with roommates beforehand. It's an unwritten rule that most renters, in a cultured city like Shanghai, respect. But the landlord let two other colleagues live with us without any suggestion of how long they planned to stay. When we had a disagreement not two weeks later, the two of them moved out almost immediately, but there was an awkward energy between me and the landlord after that.

J and S had already left the shop by this point. So, at work I was stuck with D and W stealing things behind my back, and the wedge this drove between us. As long as they kept up the thefts, and I didn't take part, they were never going to see me as one of them, even if I never intended to snitch. They were no match for J and S anyway, not in terms of their expertise or their moral and personal integrity. J and S had been straightforward, dependable guys. J was a veteran technician who loved riding bikes—road bikes, mountain bikes, street bikes, he rode them all. S was a tech nerd, who preferred tinkering with bikes to riding them. He moonlighted as a "mountain roadster," which basically means he rode a modified mountain bike on city roads, purely to join in on the fun. They were the sort of people I wanted to get to know.

D and W, on the other hand, were slippery customers. I got the impression they could have been up to anything. D, the "single-speedster," was a fan of retro road bikes with skinny-tube frames, but he was no technician. W had had his own bike shop in his hometown, but when the business didn't take off, he moved to Shanghai to find a job where he could level up his skills and technical knowledge. He studied under J and S in his early days at the shop. Neither of them were bad people, really. In fact, I'd say they were about average based on my experience, and I'm sure a lot of cyclists would have said they were more friendly than Y.

After D and W left—D after a fight with Y, and W when Y fired him due to disagreements over work arrangements—the new hires that Y brought on board all had plenty of their own problems. Some of them even had sticky fingers, like their predecessors. So, it wasn't long before Y invited S back to help out for a few months, since he had become a recluse after quitting and couldn't find a new job. Then, he left again. Y had wanted him back because of how uncomplicated he was to manage: He loved nothing more than obsessing over the technical aspects of bikes and didn't need as much pay as J.

I was the shop's most senior full-time employee by now, even though I had only worked there for all of a year. Y asked my opinion, in private, about promoting me to trainee manager. I still remembered the bind that J found himself in after going down a similar path, so I quickly refused. To be honest, the shop's staff were no longer people I could hope to manage. Neither Y nor I understood the technical side of the job beyond a basic theoretical knowledge. We couldn't do any of the hands-on work ourselves, and with me and her at the head we would still have had to depend on the technicians for the shop to be functional. As far as I can tell, industry outsiders managing industry insiders is a recipe for disaster—this was one critical area where we couldn't compensate for one another's shortfalls. Not to mention Y's working methods alone were guaranteed to create friction with the new employees. There were signs of conflict already on the horizon, and I was too soft a character to do anything about it. I could anticipate the dynamic becoming even more painful and unhappy than it was before, and that meant interminable days ahead spent stuck between a rock and a hard place.

What made me feel worse, though, was how Y was always so industrious. She had long slept only four or five hours a night, and threw herself into her work every day like it was the last thing she was going to do. Yet her employees seemed intent on foiling her, and even her regular dinner invitations couldn't win them around to doing things her way. But again, they weren't bad people overall, they weren't even difficult to get along with. Yet, I heard from more than one source that people found Y to be a headache. She was often at the brand HQ trying to coordinate situations and secure her interests, and people there shrank when they saw her coming.

She didn't have a great reputation among cyclists. She was too much of a hustler, too driven, and people said it came off as greedy; her interest in the bike shop being solely business-related, they felt like she was an invasive opportunist more than she was one of them. But she wasn't well-off by any stretch of the imagination, and the money she had was earned through hard work, not from wealthy parents. I was helpful to her, in that context, because we were quite alike—I wasn't part of the cycling scene and had no preconceptions about her—and I would talk business during business hours, instead of my passion for bikes; just purely how to beat the competition. I did as I was told and worked hard without complaint. She was more at ease working with me than with anyone else. But the bad outweighed the good in determining how I felt in the end. It was only a matter of time before she was drawn into a fight with the whole team, and I'd be the one caught in the middle. Then, there'd be no pleasing anyone.

Y had a complicated way of looking at certain things, but she couldn't have been simpler in how she saw others. It sometimes left me dumbfounded. Like the time she asked if I was looking for another job. I told her I wouldn't as long as I was staying in Shanghai, and she started pushing me to find myself a girlfriend in the city. She even tried her hand at playing matchmaker.

Around the start of summer, I handed in my resignation to Y and prepared to leave Shanghai. To get me to stay, she made some promises that I knew would only backfire, because she never hashed out the conditions beforehand. Anyway, even if I had been willing to offer myself up for the cause, I wasn't equipped to cope with the bind she would find herself in if she carried on. It seemed about time that she try a different way of operating. She might have started by picking a partner who had technical know-how.

I have had lots of employers, and I have left many jobs. My time in Shanghai was, to some extent, just a repetition of previous work experiences. Instead of moving forward, I fell, time and again, into the same situations. Most of my bosses really liked me, because of a few qualities in particular. But they all gradually wore me down until I couldn't go on, and I left. A post I put on my WeChat Moments around that time might make for a suitable end to this chapter:

> "Life is an upward spiral." It's a vivid image, whoever said it first. But it gives no notion of how slowly this upward motion occurs—by only the smallest degrees, at an almost imperceptible pace. Past lives are always repeating, as are the people who feature in them. All that changes are their names and appearances. Individuality is a myth; all we have that is unique to us are our relationships with others. Relationships that repeat. When your new girlfriend starts to seem more and more like your last girlfriend, know that it's not because they are all that similar as people, but that their having been your girlfriend has shaped them, bringing out certain facets of their personalities. Like two actors playing the same character in different films—their performances are going to share some things in common. Own this fact, and you'll know what to expect from your next beau. In fact, you met her when you met your first

girlfriend ever. The same goes for the new company you've just started at, and your new boss there, and colleagues—soon you'll see them becoming like your previous bosses and workmates, and you'll know what experience awaits you just around the corner. These are all just actors and settings in your life. A series of stacked circles of different sizes, with you as their axis, spiraling upwards—some of them line up, others don't. But it's no wonder that people envy the simple-minded for not being able to see beneath the surface of life, to this essence of things. For them, every day is a new day, and every person they meet a stranger. They get to experience the same pain and joy, over and again, untold times, each time as if it were the first.

4

Other Jobs I've Had

My First Job to My Eighth

My very first job was as a waiter in a hotel. My school organized internships for students before they graduated, and this was one of them. It might not count as official employment, but I did as much work every day as anyone else there. My salary was six hundred yuan per month, if I remember right, though I assume this was after the school had taken its cut. I was sent to a four-star hotel, with thirty or forty other students from two classes in my grade. I started in the banquet department, but concierge or room service would have been better deals. There, it turned out, waiters got tips. In banquets, all we got was tired, though this didn't really bother me at the time. I found the whole experience of work to be novel enough that it satisfied a lot of my previous curiosity and fascination with society.

I wasn't a great student, I didn't get along with studying, so school had always felt like it was holding me back. None of my classes interested me in the slightest. But this never occurred to me as something to worry about, since the same went for most students at my school. Also, my grades somehow still put me in the top three achievers in my class. Then, during the internship, I discovered that a lot of my classmates disliked working as much as they disliked school, whereas I felt the opposite. At least, I liked it more than them.

One moment that stands out in my memory was when we were clearing the banquet hall, moving the chairs and tables, and my classmates ganged up on me, making jokes, because I'd stacked more chairs than them. The list of jobs never ends, they said, work quickly and they'll only give you more to do. You're not allowed a break until the end of the day, anyway.

These classmates were annoyed because, if *I* tried hard, the head waiter would hold them to the same standard. Looking back now, I can see that they were probably complaining about me without my knowledge even before then. I was naïve and a people pleaser, friendly to everyone. So I listened to what they said and tried my best to ease off the work when I was with them. This was no skin off my back. As a young twenty-year-old, I wasn't as sensitive to the intricacies of social interactions as I eventually became. I think the reason I still remember this particular experience after all these years is because I would go on to have so many others just like it. These experiences accumulated, and only slowly started to take hold and shape me further down the line, making me feel more and more that dealing with people was a struggle.

The internship lasted six months: I spent two months in the banquet department, and the rest in the Western-style restaurant. The banquet department, as the name suggests, hosted various kinds of dinner events. There were two large dining halls and several rooms. The smaller private rooms could hold one table apiece, versus the twenty-odd each that the halls could fit. The hotel being state funded, and so belonging to the municipal government, these spaces were often used for official department conferences. Businesses also rented them for product launches or promotional events. We laid out the tables and seating according to different events' needs, rearranging them after almost every one. This involved clearing and replacing all of the twenty-plus tables, hundreds of chairs, and thousands of items of tableware. To remove the two-meter-diameter round tables, we stood them on their sides and rolled them into storage. The chairs we stacked and wheeled out on a platform trolley. There was even a knack to changing the tablecloths by first collecting the fresh cloth into both hands, then casting it over the table as if it were a fishing net. It was one I never quite perfected, and the employees weren't going to waste time helping temporary interns work on their skill set. So we were mostly lumped with simple tasks like laying the glasses and plates, and moving the tables and chairs. Setting up for government department conferences was the only time we really had to pay attention to details, working in twos with a length of nylon string to make sure that the tables, chairs, and crockery were perfectly in line. If it was a normal banquet, after setting up, we went to the kitchen to help with serving or stayed in the room to attend to guests.

Two months in, I transferred to the Western-style restaurant, which occupied one wing of the third floor, the restaurant in the other wing being Chinese. The banquet rooms were on the floor above. The Western restaurant was only as big as one of the larger banquet rooms, if that. Business wasn't great either. But this didn't mean us staff were any less busy—there were too few of us to keep up.

Lunch and dinner were self-service, while in the mornings and afternoons, we served dim sum along with the Chinese restaurant. That's four sittings every day. We also provided the twenty-four-hour room service, for which the male waiters were on rotating night shifts. I actually preferred working nights, even back then. I could take things at my own pace without a supervisor breathing down my neck.

Guangdong-style dim sum is sometimes called "morning tea," but the focus is more on the savory and sweet bites than on the tea drinking. The customers were mostly elderly folk who didn't eat much, or spend much money. Really, they just came to pass the time. But Saturday mornings were a different story. Often, it was a full house, with a line out the door. In the afternoons, we had all sorts of people come in: to talk business, to rest their weary legs after some shopping, to see friends.

Unlike most hotel restaurants at the time, which were contracted out, ours was still run by the hotel. But this wasn't the reason we weren't doing so well. The issue was we were on the third floor rather than street level. There were no smartphones then, brick phones weren't even in wide use yet, so building a reputation really was a matter of word of mouth. Nobody could find us on an app and read our reviews. This meant our customer base was reduced to regulars, who lived or worked nearby, and hotel guests from the upper floors.

Not to mention we were far from experts in the cuisine we purported to serve. We couldn't have prepared a steak, even if a customer demanded one. We did do fries and spaghetti Bolognese, which *are* "Western," but there were also udon noodles and other Japanese fare on the menu, and local dishes like beef stir-fry with rice noodles and Yangzhou fried rice. It was a hodgepodge, frankly, and none of it done particularly well. You could say that people traveled from neither far nor wide to sample our buffet. The manager didn't mind, though. He was just another worker doing his job. Plus, the more food left over at the end of the day, the better the pickings for us. It might have been sitting in stainless steel trays keeping warm for two to three hours, desiccating, but it was made with good-quality ingredients and still smelled appetizing. It would have been a shame to throw it away. Some colleagues even brought their own lunchboxes to fill and take home.

We always ate at the hotel canteen afterward, regardless how stuffed we were. We were not going to miss out on the one free meal staff was allowed a day. Our classmates in the concierge and room service departments would also be there. When they saw how much tastier the buffet grub looked than the comped meals, they would beg us to save them some leftovers. "We will when you save us some of your tips!" we loved to reply. It made them furious. But we weren't without opportunity for tips ourselves. We sometimes got them taking meals up to guests' rooms. This was another reason why I liked working the night shift so much. There would be three of us on: the chef responsible for making the dishes, and two waiters who accepted orders over the phone, delivered food to rooms, and settled bills. If there were no orders, we just chatted while folding napkin pyramids to save the day workers some time. When it got quiet after midnight, we took turns napping.

At the end of the six-month internship, we could choose whether we wanted to stay on and become employees, or leave.

Most of us left. The head of HR was a woman called Pan, who everyone referred to as Director. The title was a holdover from when the hotel was still state owned. She, in particular, regretted my decision to go. She regularly wandered around the hotel, checking in on us interns; I must have made an impression on her. But the Western restaurant manager ruined the place for me. I thought he was a foulmouthed lout. My classmates, though, were desperate to get in good with him. Their behavior toward this lowly restaurant manager with no real authority verged on flattery. Yet, the most he could do for them was reduce how much they appeared in the work schedule, or maybe just forget about them entirely. But these classmates apparently saw sucking up to your superiors as an essential stepping stone into the real world. It turned me rebellious—my disdain for the students, I mean—but it was the manager who was on the receiving end, as if he had corrupted them somehow. In reality, he'd done nothing to put me out and could do very little to control my classmates' fawning. But I still acted cold towards him and made it clear I didn't think much of the man. I was very childish.

My second ever job was as an assistant in a clothing store opened by a Hong Konger down a pedestrianized street. The store sold clothing for the niche South Korean brand Moon Goon. The brand's signature was this tribal pattern that looked like stylized tendrils of fire, with a gothic font, all in black, white, or red. At the time, it was expensive for what it was: A single short-sleeved shirt might cost two to three hundred yuan. The boss had a partner in Dongguan whom she employed to make copies of the clothing based on the genuine stuff she imported from Korea. Half of our stock was fake. The knock-offs were significantly worse quality, but more because of the materials than the workmanship. I wasn't there too long before it became easy to tell with a look which clothes were produced in South Korea and which in Dongguan. But the brand was so little known in China that most of our customers had never heard the name before, never mind knew enough to notice the difference. And indeed, what *is* the difference between fake and real for a brand nobody has heard of?

I was among the store's first hires. Very quickly, I became aware I wasn't cut out for a sales job. I was a passive server—I answered customers' questions and fetched them what they wanted, but I never tried to change anyone's mind. I lacked the resilience to take a "no" in stride, so I just didn't ask. The slightest whiff of resistance, and I threw in the towel. It's a wonder the store didn't fire me, given I sold the least of everyone.

It was not only persuading customers to part with their money that I struggled with; I also couldn't bring myself to compete over sales. So if a customer entered when both myself and a colleague were free, I simply stood aside. I couldn't handle friction, let alone full-blown conflict. It was partly why I was always polite and respectful, and made sure to get along with all my colleagues, even when they were at war. Maybe, to them, I was just a harmless weirdo with no ambitions of my own, content just to watch, or a happy imbecile with no idea what he was doing there.

Regardless, the manager kept me around. In fact, I might have been her favorite. Seeing as I was no good at sales, she just assigned me to the stockroom, which already had someone managing it. But after I started in there, this colleague began helping out on the shop floor more and turned out to be a much better salesperson than I ever could have been. Still, when the store decided to select five employees to give insurance, under pressure from a recent government initiative, the manager unexpectedly picked me, the worst performer, which flattered me enormously. But I noticed that this galled some of my colleagues. Knowing I needed to keep working alongside them, I decided the insurance wasn't worth the potential trouble. I tactfully declined the manager's nice offer, saying it wouldn't be good for the unity of the store.

This was twenty years ago now, back when I had no notion of individual rights. My parents had only ever taught me to be kind to others. They failed to mention I also had to stick up for my own interests. If I could go back, I wouldn't be so foolish again. Today, I would accept without a qualm. This is the lawful right of every worker, not a favor bestowed by capitalists. And if one's colleagues don't like it, they have to take it up with the management. Their grievance isn't with me. If they have forgotten that, then I am more than willing to give them a friendly reminder. It really is that simple, yet I didn't see this back then. Maybe because nobody had ever sat me down to talk it through before. My parents wouldn't go near the topic. They had spent their whole lives in the same work units; the market economy was completely alien to them. They grumbled endlessly when my school stopped organizing employment for us, yet spoke about so-and-so in their unit who was dealing stocks, in an almost exasperated tone, as if that person was on a one-way track to prison for profiteering.

This was in part due to the general level of knowledge in society at the time, as our perspectives on anything tend to be. Had it been a wider concern and point of discussion, then maybe this would have prompted my parents to learn more about it for themselves. But this was an era when access to information was limited. Not everyone had the internet, for one. So, often, we could only talk about many of the issues that affected us based on what we learned from the people around us. The thing was, my family was from out of town and had no relatives that lived nearby. My parents are unsociable folk, too. Especially my dad. He was from farming stock, unsuited to city life, and didn't have a single friend he could confide in at work. We struggled even for people to call in on during Spring

Festivals. Often it wasn't until almost the Lantern Festival, near the end of the holiday, that a colleague or two of my mother's might squeeze in a visit from us, by which point there would only be the least tasty of the candies left in their treat boxes.

It is no surprise that I seemed to be the most naïve and immature, as well as the slowest, of all my classmates when I finally joined the world of work for myself, even though I had been no different from them at school. It was night and day between what I was like in my student days and afterward. I watched my classmates change almost the moment they left, and the gap between them and me only widened with time, our differences setting deeper in us. Meanwhile, this seemingly natural transformation continued to elude me. How they went from students to full-blown grown-ups just like that was a mystery. I questioned whether there had been an adult version of them hidden inside their adolescent selves all along. They only needed to shed their student skins and the metamorphosis was complete. Yet inside me there had only ever been a student. I was the onion that would remain an onion no matter how many layers were peeled away; destined never to be the citrus fruit, who just under the skin has a sweet and juicy pulp.

I am taking such pains to explain this because I'm afraid, otherwise, that today's readers won't be able to understand how I could have been so stupid. I am stumped myself. So I feel like I have to assure the incredulous that I really was that dumb. It's embarrassing. However, I am bolder now. I believe the store really was rewarding me for my work, not only paying for my social security because it had to. I also see that I deserved it. In fact, I speak highly of myself often in this book, with an easy conscience, without awkwardness. I'm just not that kid anymore, always seeking to prove myself, taking hits on purpose so people don't think I'm being somehow duplicitous. I eventually realized that trying to get everyone to like me was a blind and futile impulse. We all project ourselves onto others—but know there's no way you can ever convince anyone of your own sincerity. Better still, there is no need to even try with anyone who is sincere themselves.

When I eventually quit the store, the manager was upset. It's strange to say, really, because she had no good reason to be. I had made no promises and was at liberty to leave when I wanted. As I see it, she had treated me well and thought, even if I didn't bow down and swear fealty, I should at least show my thanks by staying and being a trustworthy assistant, helping her through the hard times and building the business with her. Plus, I was in no position with my qualifications to turn my nose up at the job, modest though it was. Her looking out for me had always been so I would stay. She assumed I understood this, when in reality I didn't. I knew very little about anything—I was callow, not a mind reader.

It is clear to me looking back that the manager was highly ambitious. She owned shares in the store, so was more than just a worker there. If she could make the business successful, the

Hong Kong owner was likely to invest in a second and maybe a third location, and she would probably gain a key role in the company. I was valuable to her because I was straightforward. I wasn't greedy, which was rare, and I was humble and kind, dependable, the precise opposite of everyone else she hired. I was the weakest when it came to sales ability, no question there, but maybe in her view, competent people were a dime a dozen—she was highly competent herself. Trust is what's hard to come by.

I quit to go to night school, which I couldn't attend when I had to work until 10 P.M. I didn't tell the manager this was the reason, I've forgotten why; maybe I worried she would try persuading me that college was a waste of time and money. I wasn't in the habit of saying no to others, especially when people seemed to have my best interests at heart. But I know now that she would have been right. I learned nothing of value at night school, and this wasn't entirely my fault. I had worked at the clothing store for over half a year.

For my third job, I was an attendant at a Petroleum and Chemical Corporation gas station. I found the job in the classifieds and started out as non-staff personnel, outside the regular payroll. I took a pay cut from just over 2,000 yuan at the clothing store to 1,800. The station had eight pumps, arranged in back-to-back pairs, on islands. It sold ninety-octane gasoline, ninety-seven-octane gasoline, and zero-sulfur diesel fuel. My first day there, my colleagues said nothing to me the whole time, besides showing me how to operate the pumps. I remember going over to help a taxi driver who had just pulled up, and he gave me the side-eye like I was some hustler. I asked politely if he wanted ninety- or ninety-seven-octane gasoline, and his mystifying response was, "What do you think?"

Nobody had cared to tell me that cabdrivers generally filled their cars themselves, out of distrust, in case we pulled some stunt. The most my colleagues offered them when they drove into the station was an icy stare, before checking if they had paid. But I didn't know this yet. I only later learned that a cab would never take ninety-seven-octane gasoline. My question, from where he was standing, was idiotic, and also implied a hidden agenda.

I soon knew that even if gas attendants and cabdrivers were not mortal enemies, they were far from being friends. Work was tough for the drivers, a lot didn't go their way, so they vented their anger on us. The people who created the injustices were not worth provoking. If gas prices rose by even one tenth of a yuan, we were the ones who felt the sharp end of their barbs, as if we had a hand in it, the extra money going to fill our pockets. And to be fair, we didn't treat them all that differently.

The moral of this story: When disgruntled, the lowly among us only have each other to pick on, because going after the powerful will only cost us in the end. And if that's too much, there are always animals.

Love is blind, people like to say. But if you ask me, love sees clearest of all; it is the least interested in personal gain, and the most true to itself. What's blind is hatred.

We worked a three-shift pattern at the station. Every time we changed our shift—between the morning, afternoon, or night—we had one day off. We must have rotated once per week. The attendants were divided into four teams of four. I can still picture the three colleagues in mine now, three women for whom I was the obligatory male teammate. Most of the staff were women. I couldn't say if this was common or just particular to our filling station.

So, cabdrivers didn't trust us not to try to scam them, like I said. But really, they didn't need to. Most of them came in every day and knew the pumps as well as we did, and they minded every *fen* they spent. Not all customers were so safe from my team's schemes, though. Whether the same went for other teams, or even other filling stations, I don't know. Government agency drivers at the time would pay for gas with coupons rather than cash, and were often careless enough to leave us alone with the car after they had parked and barked their instructions our way. To be fair, the vehicle wasn't theirs. When drivers did this, my teammates would spring to action, working together to hide how much fuel they added, then pocket more of the coupons for themselves. I didn't know anything about this at first; they probably thought I was too stupid to involve in their schemes, or that I would give the game away, but eventually one of them was caught. Strangely, the driver didn't punish her beyond a scolding. He didn't even attempt to get the extra coupons back. But again, they will have been state issued, so what did it matter to him how many he used? He was more concerned my colleagues thought they could swindle him, which he regarded as an insult. Anyway, we exchanged the coupons my colleagues managed to steal for money for our team activities. This was part of the reason I wasn't innocent; not just because I didn't report my teammates, but because, more than once after finding out what was going on, I still went to morning tea with them. How easily one corrupts.

I had worked at the gas station three, maybe four months when a group of company heads arrived for an inspection. After receiving a rundown from the manager of how things were going, they took us through the new regulation language for talking with customers. The old hands that were my colleagues must have decided this was all just for show, and gave only perfunctory performances, whereas I lamely did exactly as I was told, to the very best of my ability.

It turned out that the heads had come to find candidates for a new assignment. The company planned to make a new gas station on the fringes of the city into a model station, and shoot a short film there for internal use to illustrate standard practices. My scrupulous performance had earned me a role.

Though I'm sure it helped more than a little that I was the youngest of my colleagues, who were all in their thirties or forties, and also the tallest and most energetic. The best of a bad bunch? The tallest of a short bunch? Either way, in the eyes of the bosses, I had something.

Being picked meant an immediate transfer to a different station. While the one I was at was only around a mile from home, and a little farther away from my night school, this other station was several miles out, with bad transport links. The company had chosen it for its new building and pumps that were not yet covered with a permanent layer of black grime. There was also a newly laid road next to the station that was even straighter, wider, flatter, and neater than the city roads. *And* it was surrounded by fields of flowers cultivated by locals, which would offer the perfect backdrop for the shoot, free of charge—Big Garden was actually the name of the area, and, yes, the station was Big Garden Gas Station. Customers might not have been queueing up somewhere so out of the way, but this did leave plenty of spare time for rehearsing and filming.

Our station manager didn't want to see me go, but there was nothing she could do until the company assignment was complete, when she would immediately apply for a retransfer, she assured me. In the short time I'd been at the station, I had already received the employee of the month award once. Her picking me hadn't gone down well with colleagues who had been there longer, but maybe she intended me as an example for them to straighten out their attitudes. I've forgotten how much money it included, but I was terrified accepting it, and the very next day I bought a crate of iced tea for my colleagues to share.

My night school was for adult learners, most of whom had part-time or full-time jobs, so the school was very tolerant of absences. Two-thirds attendance for a course was fine. But at the new station, there was mention of military-style management—I don't know what the heads were thinking. The worst part of this was we had to stay in the company dormitories right by the station, so we could be on call at all hours. I couldn't go home or easily get to class. I would scoff at this sort of arrangement today, feigning compliance or fighting my corner, but back then . . . What took the cake was they hadn't even put me on the regular payroll yet! I was a temporary worker, on a fixed salary of 1,800 yuan, with no medical benefits, and they had the nerve to encroach on my private life? They hadn't asked if I wanted to move in the first place, as if I'd just obey, regardless. Militaristic was the right word for it, but I hadn't signed on to be a soldier. This situation wasn't uncommon, though. People lacked a general awareness of their rights in those days, and the labor laws weren't as refined as they are now. Still, I'm not saying there was malicious intent from the bosses; they possibly hadn't considered it an infringement. And more than feeling angry, I was anxious that I would fail to meet the company's expectations and cause problems for the rest of the team.

Looking back now, I can see the situation as clear as day, but at the time I had no idea what to do. There was no one I could talk to. My parents had old-fashioned, conservative mindsets and already felt unsettled by the dramatic changes occurring in society and at work. They were isolated themselves, struggling—with money and with understanding and accepting this new world; no wonder they had so little time for me. I had also avoided discussing anything with them since I became an adult, because they never knew how to provide a fitting solution. All of my decisions had been my own since the day I joined society—maybe that's why I've never fully integrated. They basically haven't given me a single good piece of advice ever, or any help beyond the money they lent me once for starting a business. But equally, they never required that I make millions and bring honor to the family name, or take care of them in old age. They only asked that I respect the law and not be a source of trouble for others or society. I see now that I should have simply spoken with the new gas station's bosses, explained to them about night school, and requested concessions. I'm sure they weren't unreasonable people. At the very least, they would have been able to recognize that studying is not a bad thing, and it wouldn't affect my work. What's more, I had started at the school before they assigned me to the new station; if they really couldn't relax the rules for me, they could have still let me go back to my original post. But I didn't have the confidence to negotiate conditions—that would have meant favoritism and special treatment, and would have upset my colleagues again. In reality, I was overthinking it.

For the two months I stayed at the new station, I would sneak to and from class whenever the bosses weren't around, but I still missed a lot of lessons. Seeing as I couldn't meet the station's requirements, I decided the only thing to do was to quit. I had been with the company for six months. Very few people my age would have chosen to work in a gas station. My colleagues there were either migrant workers or older locals whose lack of specialist skills limited their employment options. In fact, a classmate of mine had been hired for the job at the same time as me, then never turned up to register. Many of us born in the city had better prospects, and had our dignity to think about—plenty of people saw gas jockeying as lowly work. They might have claimed that "professionalism doesn't discriminate between class," but that's not really what they believed. My parents did, though, wholeheartedly. They also had no other family or friends in the city, so they didn't need to trouble themselves with saving face. When they first heard I was going to work in a gas station, they were genuinely happy for me.

My fourth job was doing deliveries for a Chinese-style fast-food chain. I worked for two and a half hours every lunchtime. The fast-food joint provided lunch, but there was no base pay.

My income depended entirely on completed orders. The commission for a successful delivery was 1.5 yuan, and the most orders I could manage in a shift was twenty. It was part-time work really, but my previous three jobs had all clashed with night school, and I was struggling to find a good nine-to-five because of how bad my grades were. I stuck it out at the fast-food place for half a year before a classmate referred me for another job, and I quit.

My fifth job was working for a popsicle wholesaler. A classmate's family ran it from a marketplace next to a shantytown. Before starting, I thought I would be responsible for delivering goods to clients, but that turned out to be only partly true. I also had to find the clients in the first place. In effect, I was a salesperson. Every day, I toured the nearby supermarkets and convenience stores, looking for empty freezers, and if I saw one I asked the staff what they needed, then delivered it. That was, if I could beat my competition to the punch—my competition being the other full-time employee and numerous part-timers in the role. But I didn't feel up to the challenge. I was already conflicted about social interaction, slow to pick up on the true intent behind others' words, and when I eventually did catch on, I only ever felt annoyed or embarrassed. This happened enough that I started to instinctively keep people at arm's length, even those I had grown fond of. Haggling was not a strength of mine, either. Talking profit and thrashing out details didn't come naturally to me. In my head, it was like I was trying to offend people. This only sent my people-pleasing into overdrive and worsened my social anxiety. People-pleasing, in a backward way, made me fear getting close with anyone, because the result was always just further disappointment and frustration.

Acts of selflessness, I had found, tended to bring out people's greed rather than their kindness. During my internship at the hotel, we used to work split shifts: four hours in the morning and four in the evening, for example. None of us liked it, since it meant spending more time and money on commuting than we would for a consecutive eight-hour shift. Some people lived far away and struggled to go home in between, so could only wait around killing time or take aimless strolls in the nearby area while the second part of the day began. This was why the head waiter made sure everyone got the same number of split shifts every month. He was trying to be fair.

Then, one day, a colleague asked if I could swap with her, because she had something to do at home—a split shift for one of my ordinary shifts. She would return the favor later, she promised. But swapping back and forth like that seemed like a lot of extra trouble for nothing, so I told her not to worry about it. When she asked why, I said there was no difference for me between the two types of shift; I didn't have anything to do after work regardless. But this isn't what I really meant: I disliked the split shifts just as much as everyone else, I only wanted to assure her the request was okay. Apparently, this was naïve. A few days later, she asked if I would swap again, but not because she had something to do at home. Instead, she said, straight up, "If you think there's no difference, let's just switch. I don't like the split shifts." I was blindsided. How was I supposed to refuse her? Tell her I had lied before and, like her, hated the split shifts? I couldn't bring myself even to do that, so I simply agreed. Of course, it didn't end there. Some days later, another colleague who had caught wind asked if I'd cover for them . . .

Thankfully, a classmate eventually came to my rescue. He bawled out the first official employee I'd exchanged with, and the two of them got into an argument. My classmate accused her of being shameless, and she told him to mind his own business. Meanwhile, I stood off to the side, dying from awkwardness, scared I had ruined the peace. But nobody asked to trade shifts again.

I was so very meek back then, a yes-man, terrified that I always seemed to react to things totally differently from everybody else. Gradually, it occurred to me "everybody else"—though not really—saw things exclusively from their own perspective. I'm not saying I was so bighearted that I never complained. Just, I let my grievances and disappointments pile high until they spilled over into irritability and anger. If I didn't want to keep losing out, I had to stop people from taking advantage of me, either by becoming like everybody else and playing their games—go tit for tat in selfishness and greed—or pushing people out as best I could. For me, the second option was by far the easiest.

So, by the time I was selling popsicles to make a living, I had put up barriers between myself and the world around me. Clients I had dealt with numerous times I still approached as if we were strangers whenever I stopped by, greeting them in an overly polite way, making small talk. They must have been baffled: This kid can't have forgotten me already, can he? I was oblivious to how this standoffish behavior might hurt people's feelings. In my wishful imagination, what kept the world turning was fairness and rationality, rules—not human emotions. People didn't need affection, only a mutual respect for protocol, then they could handle anything effectively, and everybody could lead a comfortable and satisfying life.

I was shyer now than when I had recently graduated, but my social anxiety hadn't spiraled into a disorder yet. It was to become more complex first, then worsen, shaped by many other factors besides those I've already mentioned. I was deeply afraid of disappointing people, for one. If someone gave a compliment, I reflexively jumped to denial and scrambled to lower myself. I feared that, sooner or later, they would discover I wasn't all they had made me out to be. I preferred that they thought very little of me, from the start. That sense of crisis, that at any moment they might see through whatever small good I represented, was excruciating. And if somebody insisted on flattery—though few people did—I would remove myself from their life. This way, I abandoned them before they could abandon me.

There was no rationale behind this strategy, it was a spontaneous defense mechanism. People like to say that our character determines our fate, but I say that words like fate and destiny feel too big for the times we live in, whereas character plays a not inconsiderable role in determining the course of a person's life. When I share my stories about work, I find it impossible not to discuss it. Many of the decisions I made were influenced by my character rather than any balanced assessment of the pros and cons. If I don't tell readers who I am, they might struggle to understand some of my past responses and choices.

I scraped by at the popsicle wholesaler for some months, too self-conscious to even call what I was doing a job because I hardly earned more there than I had doing two and a half hours at the fast-food place. That was working nine to five. But the job was, at least, flexible, in the sense there was no need to clock in or out, and skipping the occasional inclement day was fine.

I covered the area on my bike, all the alleyways and the nooks and crannies in the neighboring shantytown. Some stores were down back alleys that were barely a yard wide. Still, my main competition was always one step ahead of me, and more often than not I arrived at stores to find their freezers full. My problem was, while he had a cell phone, I only had a pager, and I never told the store owners the number. He had also worked the area for longer and established relationships with most of the businesses, so when stock was running low, he was the one they would call. I was left with any he missed along the way. It helped that I wasn't desperate to make money yet. I still had to study in the evenings, so I told myself that the real work would begin once I graduated, for now I could see this as an extra on the side. When the weather started to get cold some months in, and popsicles harder to sell, there eventually came the day I didn't make a single sale—I couldn't face continuing after that.

My sixth job was another classmate referral. I never asked any of these classmates to help me out, they offered themselves. Again though, this job wasn't all that official. We didn't sign a contract, and the hours weren't strict. For our workspace, the boss rented an apartment in a residential complex. The product was 3D architectural renderings. The boss handled the business side of things and sales, and the drawings were all done by the single employee, a relative of his. I was hired as an apprentice, with a salary of six hundred yuan, lunch included. I still remember the software editions we used to this day: AutoCAD 14, 3ds Max 4, and Photoshop 5.5.

I hadn't been there a week when two more apprentices joined, a man and a woman, both of them referred by friends of the boss. Since the designer was so busy, we had to teach ourselves, with books and CDs, and only interrupted him with questions if we hit upon a problem.

Photoshop was only very basic in those days, and I soon got the hang of it again based on previous experience. AutoCAD was pretty straightforward too. Its essential operations were learnable in a day, but would take much longer to master. And without any foundation, even just wrapping my head around the full-size architectural drawings was a stretch. Of the three programs, 3ds Max was the most challenging to use, for one, because it was in English, but also because the sheer amount of possible instructions was overwhelming, and it only multiplied with each new plug-in we added.

I was at this place for around half a year, before leaving along with the other male apprentice. We were in the same grade at my night school, me in advertising and him in financial accounting. Every day after work, we headed straight to the school together, for classes, eating a lunch box of rice or rice noodles on the way. We called it quits at the job because we both came to the conclusion our boss was too shrewd, especially when money was involved. Both of us were losing out by doing cheap work for him. We had no security or guarantees of our rights, his workspace wasn't registered after all, so we relied entirely on his good conscience. And his was not a conscience I trusted all that much . . . The older brother of the classmate who referred me knew the boss, for instance, and had said before I started that the salary for apprentices was a thousand yuan. But at the end of my first month there, I only got six hundred. I didn't know what I'd done wrong, and I felt too awkward to ask—not the boss or that classmate's brother. So I was useless after all, I told myself, I only got in the way, took up one of his computers, ate his rice boxes. Kicking up a fuss over a few hundred yuan was no way to thank him. But some months in, when I started to be able to contribute, and sometimes worked until midnight with the rest of the team to meet a deadline, I still went home at the end of the month with only six hundred yuan. The other guy apprentice was in a similar boat. But the cowards we were, we didn't dare take it up with the boss. We were graduating from night school soon and both figured it was time we found professions that fitted our different expertise.

Except, that's not at all what I did.

The publisher of a comic book I bought whenever it released an issue put out a call for apprentice applications. The publisher had some prestige nationally, so I thought I would give it a try. I drew a short piece, as requested, and mailed it in, never expecting that I would be chosen. Again, it's questionable how much of a job this was, since there was no pay, we only got room and board. But I worked there for the better part of a year, so I'm calling it job number seven.

The publisher rented several apartments in a residential complex. The chief editor was a Hong Konger who couldn't yet have been thirty years old. He had us all refer to him as "Teacher"—*Laoshi*. He had studied art in Japan on his own dime, then returned to start a company: a comics publisher that ran journals, promoted authors, and released book editions. I joined along with ten or so other apprentices; this time around, I was the oldest. I was twenty-three. So, the only people foolish enough to take on dubious apprenticeships at comic book publishers were children. But I was a late bloomer. In the years prior, I had muddled through my work and studies, in no hurry to consider what I really wanted to do, and unpressured by my parents to decide. They had always taught me to be frugal and had set a good example to follow, so my material needs remained modest—I didn't smoke, didn't drink (though I do now, in moderation), didn't buy big brands; for haircuts, I went to the five-yuan stalls on the roadside; I would cycle places if I could avoid public transport—my daily spending was minimal. Not having other family in the city, or any family friends, also meant I wasn't exposed to the fierce competition that sometimes exists between members of a generation, and neither were my parents. It gave us—me—space to drift along and not constantly strive for growth. My parents rarely monitored my grades and never paid for a tutor, but they also didn't demand that I keep up with children from other families. To them, diligence and discipline were far more valuable qualities than capability and cleverness.

Comic books are one of my few interests. Back then I mostly read Japanese serials: *Saint Seiya: Knights of the Zodiac*, *Dragon Ball*, *Ranma ½*, *Dr. Slump*, *Captain Tsubasa*, and *Slam Dunk* were some of my favorites. Our days at the publisher were spent practicing the basic skills of comic book drawing for a dozen hours on end. Exercises in shading, drawing figures and faces, copying backgrounds. *Laoshi* didn't teach us any of the techniques, he only assigned the exercises. Hatching and cross-hatching were what we practiced the most, repeatedly drawing parallel rows of straight lines with a dip pen, each one 4 centimeters long, with at most a 0.02-inch gap between them, though the narrower the better. The aim was to get all the lines the same length, and evenly spaced. We did this one exercise alone for more than four hours on most days. It was so tedious. It also felt like we were training to be comic book assistants, not artists. Probably, the idea was anything related to the creation of stories couldn't be taught, but was a matter of talent. We got the impression this was the same instruction *Laoshi* had received in Japan.

Ultimately, I didn't become a comic book artist. But I did make some important friends at the publisher. Hanging with them, I started listening to rock music: Sex Pistols, Nirvana, Nine Inch Nails, Radiohead, Pink Floyd. Like lots of young rockers, my new friends said we must rebel against society's power over us, against mainstream values' tendency to blindfold us to our individuality, against the hypocrisy and utilitarianism of the adult world. As far as I could tell, they weren't just saying this. With their encouragement, I felt bold enough to oppose some of the publishers' methods. My viewpoint wasn't all that far-fetched, but it was very idealistic.

A few of the group and I eventually left on account of how the publisher treated us. Before going, I drew a strip that satirized *Laoshi*'s mechanical approach to teaching.

I was back to looking for work, now twenty-four years old—on the older side compared with that year's college graduates—and apparently lacking the work experience to justify the age gap. Securing anything remotely better seemed an impossibility.

How lucky then that I'd never been picky. My eighth job was as a graphic designer for a startup magazine about anime.

My boss, previously the publisher of a very successful album review magazine changed focus when he saw potential for an anime-related publication. There were already lots of similar magazines on the market, most of them without a serial number. They came with a freebie CD and were sold as audiovisual media, with the magazine itself said to be supplementary. We used the same approach for our magazine.

The boss was a pretty stingy guy, but he was articulate and sounded refined. He knew how to hold forth and carried himself with confidence. He hired me because I didn't demand any particular salary. In my interview, I told him that as long as he gave me the same as everyone else doing the job, I would be happy. He paid 1,500 yuan for the whole three-month trial period. Looking back, I was very good value for the money. He must have noticed early on that I was a dutiful worker, his favorite kind it would later turn out.

We mostly used two pieces of software: Photoshop for the images and CorelDRAW for the formatting and typesetting, two programs I had already learned. At first, our editorial department included the chief editor, two editors, three graphic designers, and a Japanese translator. My tasks were mostly pretty dull, handling image after image, then sorting out the layout. But one perk was the magazines from Japan, Hong Kong, and Taiwan that I got to read in advance of their release in China. So, while everybody else in the country was reading bad-quality knockoffs, I could enjoy the latest batch of the real deal.

We put out one issue every month. In the early stages, the editors would be the busier group, then the pressure would shift onto us graphic designers. The day before the issues went to print, we always had to work through the night to get everything done. Procrastination being rife, the editors typically didn't hand over the full manuscript until the very last moment.

As well as the journal, we also produced single-book products, like Ultraman picture albums. The content sometimes violated copyright, but Japanese rights departments rarely bothered themselves with what was happening in China's pirated book market (we called it the "Second Channel"). In fact, the book market was already in decline. Though it would still be several years before smartphones became widely available, personal computers and easy internet access had quickly converted scores of print readers. It was under these circumstances that we were putting out pedestrian content and doing nothing to stand out from the umpteen other anime magazines, some of which had only released a few issues before vanishing. They just weren't as dauntless as us. Still, the boss started to think about how to cut costs. When my trial period came to an end, he made me sign a work contract. I remember reading it and experiencing this intense feeling of betrayal. I've long forgotten what the contract said, but I can guarantee that a lot of it violated the current labor laws. I didn't sign, but I also didn't immediately quit. Those precious magazines from abroad had trapped me. On top of the ones ordered in by the editorial department, I was using company channels to buy original editions that were almost impossible to get ahold of in China. Some of them were presents for friends. Besides, I got along well with colleagues, and there was a lot about the job I enjoyed.

At this point, I was still in touch with several of the friends I had made at the comic book publisher. Their flogging of society for its evils coincidentally felt like it could have been directed at much of my new boss's approach to work. I was starting to think that maybe society really was a foul place, and human nature ugly. This was unheard of for me. When I left the architectural drawings company, I hadn't been angry in the slightest. If anything, I was a little afraid of the boss. But I was starting to feel like my parents were to blame for all the rotten luck I had with people and work. They should have warned me. Their lessons on how to act had zero grounding in this world. They had said nothing about going after what I wanted, only that I should be frugal. What they told me was the wrong way to behave was exactly how everybody was behaving, and society wasn't punishing them for it but rewarding them, and not just rewarding them, *punishing* me.

The chief editor's rules about the magazine's content also went completely against the aesthetic that my friends and I shared. The publications were vapid, childish, pretentious, and hypocritical . . . They were a stain on the anime industry, a waste of paper, and an insult to the trees cut down to make them. So, after some intense discussion, we decided to head to Beijing together to lead bohemian lives. I finished my last day at work, made some simple preparations, then bought a hard-seat train ticket out of there.

My Ninth Job to My Eleventh

Of course, we didn't actually lead roving, bohemian lives in Beijing. When we first arrived, we stayed at a friend's place in Tongzhou, but soon moved into a rental apartment of our own nearby. Since we had no money, I found work at a copy shop in Bawangfen, commuting back and forth every day between Tongzhou and the more central Chaoyang. I kept the job for two months and can sum it up in a few short paragraphs.

The boss had a sales background, and I was his second employee. We had two computers and an offset printer for business cards. We offered design and production services for flyers, brochures, and promotional booklets, but printing business cards was where we made our money. The boss had deals with a few local hotels to give them express same-day service. When a call came in from a front desk, we went straight to collect the necessary customer information. Most of the time this was an existing card for use as a template for reprinting. Digital printing was already a thing in Beijing, but it was rarely used for business cards. The machines couldn't handle the 300gsm coated or specialty papers that were typical.

Mostly, we served high-flying businessmen, a lot of them from abroad—at least, there were no Chinese characters on their cards. We were able to charge quite a high fee, as a result. A box cost two hundred yuan with us, whereas if they went out to have the cards printed themselves, they would have paid thirty, at most. But then they couldn't have gotten door-to-door collection and delivery, or same-day printing. For our clientele, the hour they then spent sorting out new cards would have cost them far more in lost time than two hundred yuan. We could deliver orders made in the morning by that afternoon, and orders from the afternoon by the end of the day. Evening orders had to wait until the next morning.

The boss, who made the collections and deliveries himself, spent all day coming and going. I occasionally did runs when he couldn't. Our colleague, who was more practiced with the printer than either of us, stayed in the store. Since the boss covered our room and board, he and I didn't earn any more than 1,000 or maybe 1,200 yuan a month. The room was in a basement, but I only stayed there a few evenings altogether, because I still had the place in Tongzhou to go back to. I remember the basement room being dark and dank, with no hot water or any way of drying clothes, and there was no telling what time of day it was without a clock. Also, there was a line to use the toilet every morning.

Work basically ate up all my time for creation, which annoyed my friends. Work was how the machinery of society made slaves of us humans, they said, and when they put it like that, I felt like they had a point. But simply being alive on this planet means being enslaved in some way, shape, or form—either from this side or that—whether you work or not. Ancient Greek philosophers considered carnal desire a kind of enslavement, but then they never said anything about being able to escape from those desires—besides by getting old and dying. Still, I took my friends' advice and quit. That was my ninth job.

To save money, my friends and I decided to move even farther out of the city, from Tongzhou to the still more remote Yanjiao. We roped in two more people to join us and split the rent between five. Like Tongzhou, Yanjiao was nowhere near as developed or bustling back then as it has become, and we managed to secure an apartment with an area of over one thousand square feet. It was part of a collective housing project, funded and owned by local farmers, so the rent was inexpensive, around a hundred yuan each. But I was already broke, so I resorted to calling my parents to ask for a loan. It made no sense to them why I had chosen a life like that, and they didn't approve, but they still helped out some.

 I also lent a hand for a few days at the breakfast stall at the front of our building, working from 4 until 8 A.M. The pay was only a few yuan each time, but I could have as much breakfast as I wanted. I was in charge of deep-frying the flour dough for the *youtiao* and so spent the whole time hunched over the deep fat fryer. I could make a few hundred in a morning. Some were for selling wholesale to nearby food stores. This didn't really count as a job, though, since I earned so little pay. It's why I couldn't stay there longer.

We made a lot of unforgettable memories in Yanjiao, but our creative work never really got anywhere. My friends believed most of what was published in journals at that time to be worthless garbage—the equivalent of tamed livestock that had long lost its animal nature. But I was starting to suspect I wasn't so wild myself, anymore. Wild works couldn't be published anyway, other than circulating within underground spaces online, and that wouldn't generate the sort of income we needed to survive. We were naïve, extreme, and immature, but we were enthusiastic, and we didn't care about the consequences of our actions as long as they changed the world. I'd say, of the group, I was the more pragmatic and cooler-headed member. My friends scoffed at my perennial concern with how we were going to make money. But they were better at drawing and had far more experience in comic books than me. I had only been at the publisher for six months and completed a few dozen pages of drawing exercises. My work fell far short of publishable quality. But it was a fervent belief of theirs that, when it came to creativity, "drawing well" was the least important part. Punk music was the example they always cited—lots of punk songs use only three chords, but they still loved the music. They said that, in art, most important of all is the soul. I had soul, they said, which blew me away, because they also said that a lot of people don't. But in their visions for the future, they were living far more exciting lives than I was in my own. What I longed for most was a sense of security, and when I was around them, it was hard to avoid sometimes feeling on edge.

It is a shame that life only goes like this when you're young, and only for a very short time. Doubtless we made a lot of mistakes and messed up plenty, but those were my days of disenchantment with the world—or with society, more like. I read books then that I would never have read otherwise, and encountered ideas in them that changed my outlook and awareness. I reexamined certain values and notions that previously I simply accepted without question: what is and isn't important. This didn't happen overnight, of course, it was an ongoing process. But the seed for change was planted then and, in the years since, it has slowly and stubbornly taken root and budded. Today, it continues to grow within me, shaping me. I could swap out or erase any one of the work experiences I share in this book, and it would have no impact on who I am today. But if I didn't have this time in Beijing, I would be a very different person. If it is hyperbole to talk about rebirth, then I will say this period molded my earliest self—it gave me a fresh starting point. It no longer bothers me now if I am different from others. Instead, I cherish my individuality. I might still be ignorant and timid, but beneath that I have resilience and conviction. From then on, both work and writing became ways for me to build my spirit.

I left Beijing and stayed with my parents for several months. They didn't force me to find a job while there, probably out of fear I would return to a life of "vagrancy" if I wasn't totally happy. They wanted to care for me but didn't know how. They felt even more out of place in the big wide world than I did. They were in no position to guide me or give advice. And so, they felt ashamed.

Eventually, the boss from the anime magazine learned I was back from Beijing and jobless, so invited me to join his new company. The anime magazine had ceased operations, and he was in a new office, with a whole new staff. This latest endeavor was a periodical about audiovisual equipment, an area he was familiar with himself. Beyond this, it involved putting together the occasional themed editorial, in which most of the content would be taken from Hong Kong and Taiwanese publications or translated from Japanese. He hadn't totally given up on anime, only now he was doing children's picture books, which were low investment for quick returns.

Another project saw us turning screenshots from animated shows into comics by adding dialogue boxes. Then, there were the multimedia CDs that he advertised in his own print media and sold by mail. The content was mostly copied from online sources, so the bulk of the work revolved around collecting and organizing it according to a theme and designing the interface to be easily navigable and searchable. There were also various random side projects underway at any one time, which I won't go into here. But, basically, if we could do it, we would try. It was a scattergun approach—we did a lot, and none of it very well. From the boss's perspective, the only consolation I see this providing was it avoided waste—all manpower, space, and equipment was put to full use.

For my part, I was still taking on typesetting and graphic design tasks, but I also edited texts every now and then and, later, helped to select publication themes. Yet, despite all our efforts and combined skill, the feedback we got about our output wasn't encouraging. The products, on the whole, were middle-of-the-road, with very little to make them stand out. This was no great surprise, though—we rushed out every single one. It was the only way of surviving, releasing a nonstop stream of products. As long as we always had something new to put into retailers' hands, then we could get back the profit from the last batch of sales. There was no reason for us to try creating anything of higher quality.

The boss was also losing his patience with our distributor, who had failed to collect payments from numerous buyers. But, the distributor was the boss's younger brother-in-law and must have been brought in by the boss himself. So, even though they had some pretty nasty fights, they were stuck trying to make things work. Eventually, I found out the boss was intentionally avoiding payments. He frequently switched suppliers, citing dissatisfaction with the products or the service as the reason, just so he could avoid coughing up the final installment. He even refused to pay courier fees—these were settled monthly, so he would default on one company and simply change to using another. He did this several times in a year.

Still, as stingy as he was, he treated me well—probably because I was useful to him, or he couldn't find anyone willing to replace me. The salary was very low, but it always arrived on time. Plus, living with my parents and paying no rent, I could get by on very little.

The audiovisual equipment magazine didn't last. Print publications were becoming harder and harder to keep afloat, with readers opting to go online for their news and information. But what did it in the end was an argument between the editor and boss. Apparently, the boss, rather than pay the editor his commission, had offered him a speaker in lieu of money. The speaker was a sample from a factory that had wanted us to write a review. We must have kept it when the factory failed to pay for the placement. To be fair, we told potential clients looking to advertise in our periodical that we sold twenty thousand copies every issue, when in reality it was three thousand. But we were far from the only publication doing this. Anyway, humans, unlike trees, have a tendency to move to a new location when death threatens. The wise man does not stand under the crumbling wall, as the saying goes. And sure enough, the editor left soon after to start his own project, and took me with him since I had just quit, too. We worked together for a month before this fell apart as well, which isn't long enough for it to count as a real job, but I'll tell you a little about it, all the same.

The editor knew a guy through his business connections, whom for convenience's sake we'll just call Guy. Guy had founded an association in the neighboring D City for businesses in the automobile repair and modification industry. He reached out to the editor for help with a trade magazine, which would be mailed directly to member stores. The catch was he didn't want to spend money to run it, so he coaxed the editor into taking it on with the promise of attracting advertisers to generate revenue. Still in his twenties, the editor had a lot to learn about doing business and easily fell for Guy's elaborate sales pitch. Partly, I think this was an impulsive decision to get away from our last boss.

We realized within three weeks that something was off. Guy and his friend were taking us for a ride, dragging us along to auto repair shops for strength in numbers, and demanding I design posters for free. Meanwhile, the promised advertisers were, of course, nowhere to be seen. The most we got was a stack of supplier contacts and instructions to cold-call the numbers. The suppliers were scattered across the country, and most of them had never even heard of Guy's association, so there was zero chance they were going to buy ad space in our magazine.

Some of them even called me a scammer. It was only once we were adding the final touches to the first issue that Guy reluctantly introduced us to a few clients from his personal network. But a couple ad placements weren't nearly enough to cover our production and mailing costs. So, one evening, after yet another fruitless negotiation with Guy, the editor decided to give up, and we both slunk back to our own city, defeated.

This was around the time my father had a stroke and was admitted to the hospital. I looked after him for a while, once he was allowed home. After two months of rest, he was able to walk again using a cane, but he never regained his strength. He wasn't the same man after that.

My tenth job returned me to the world of anime, but it was to the part I hated most. The government was wielding its administrative power to shore up the national animation industry by restricting the broadcast of foreign content and subsidizing local productions. For example, there were grants for every five hundred minutes that a series showed on television, and financial aid to help with tax, location costs, and more. One explanation I heard for these too-good-to-be-true schemes was that they were essentially part of an ideological struggle to stop our children from growing up exclusively on foreign shows. There was a fear about how this would influence their values. But this didn't really ring true for me. Most of the anime that we could watch from abroad spoke to basic universal values like good and evil, truth and falsehood, beauty and ugliness, none of which had anything to do with ideological divides between countries. But I was just a lowly worker, and such big-picture questions were way above my pay grade. The company I joined had only recently been established, a typical "product of policy." And honestly, it seemed no worse that government funds reach us through these channels than flow into the restaurant industry by way of official banquets.

The company had divisions for both animation and comics. I was in the latter. The animations department used Flash to do its work, so the pictures looked rough at best, and the content was unexciting. It felt decades behind animation from America and Japan. But I knew too well that our colleagues in other studios were capable of even worse stuff, which still made it on to TV. Our boss had been in the film and television industry for many years, and boasted the connections and network to show for it, so getting his company's output aired was no challenge at all.

Unfortunately, the comics I was part of making were equally shabby. To try to earn some money on the side, I would submit my own works, anonymously. Our company would put out open calls for comics submissions, but we employees were the only ones who ever answered. We would copy the concepts wholesale from online sources—because who had time to come up with their own?—then alter the designs and superficial elements, so no one could tell. It was essentially straight-up plagiarism. But the company didn't mind, as long as we signed a copyright contract. That way, if there was ever a problem, we would be the ones responsible. I was dating a woman at the time and spending much more money than usual, so I could no longer afford to remain so squeaky-clean.

Over this period, I also started to drift apart from the friends I had made in Beijing. I just couldn't face telling them about my situation. The company I was at represented everything they abhorred, and there was no question they would hate the creations I spent every day making. I had become the very embodiment of the reactionary forces of this decaying society that they condemned in their own comics. I churned out garbage, drove out quality content, and polluted people's eyes and ears—what defense is there for that? "I had no choice; everybody is doing it." I would have only been lying to myself. I might as well have cut ties with them directly. (This was what I thought at the time, anyway, though I later realized people are always changing and growing. They might have listened to the Sex Pistols in their twenties, but they won't after thirty. Not to say the Sex Pistols are bad, just that they appeal more to twenty-year-olds.) But truly, I was incompetent. I had sullied myself in murky waters, for what? To still be living hand to mouth? My girlfriend was already unhappy with me—she had started to snap over the smallest things.

Then, an old night school classmate who lived nearby and felt similarly disillusioned by his job suggested we might be better off striking out and starting a business together. He caught me just when I was thinking about how little money working for others made me, and how massive a waste of time it had turned out to be—and I agreed immediately. After some discussion, we decided to take a trip to Vietnam for market research. Our thinking was that we could get ahead by going backwards, while bringing with us all the experiences and insights of having worked in a more developed economy. We had long missed the liftoff in China—breaking into business would be much harder there, with hardly any opportunities left that someone hadn't already thought of or tried. Whereas Vietnam was more than a decade behind, and was right then in the process of a reform and opening up of its own. Maybe we would have better luck there. So, we both quit our jobs and, through the internet, found a Liuzhou girl studying in Hanoi, who we hired to be our interpreter.

We traveled to Hanoi twice, both times taking the train to Nanning, where we changed to an older "green train" for Pingxiang on the border and crossed into the country via Friendship Pass. Our interpreter was a recent graduate and still living in the Vietnam National University dorms, so we stayed in a hostel next to the school.

Hanoi felt like stepping into the past. There was scarcely a high-rise in sight, and the storefronts were straight out of 1980s China. Ho Chi Minh would apparently have shown us a more prosperous side to the country, but we never made it south, so I couldn't say for certain. As for the remaining French architecture in Hanoi, it had seen better days; repurposed, many of the buildings looked out of place.

Our interpreter told us the canteen in the girls' school didn't clean any of the bowls beyond a wipe with a cloth, so all the Chinese students took in their own lunch boxes and cutlery. She also explained that the limes the staff left on the table at the streetside joint where we ate rice noodles weren't for flavor, but for disinfecting our bowls and chopsticks. I didn't know if she was joking or not, but I still quickly squeezed lime onto both and gave them a thorough scrub.

Prices were cheap in Hanoi. An egg banh mi from a breakfast stall cost the equivalent of 3.5 yuan and could just about fill me up. Banh mi was like the Vietnamese *youtiao*, in that it could be found everywhere.

We also dipped into a French cathedral, which had a small store next to it that sold roughly hewn seashell earrings to tourists, along with old American military trinkets: lighters, canteens, dog tags. The dealer claimed these had been dug up from old battlefields, though who knows if this was true? The Vietnam War had ended more than thirty years ago.

When it came to what we planned to do, we were limited by our funds and knew we couldn't go into the trading business. The original idea had been to see if we could try our hands at retail, but after wandering around Hanoi and consulting some Chinese students there, we still couldn't come up with anything viable.

Although Hanoi was indeed a decade or more behind most Chinese cities, doing business there was not as simple as "traveling back in time to build our empire," as we'd imagined it would be. For one, imported goods were subject to tariffs, increasing costs. Also, we didn't speak or read the language, so we would have to rely on an interpreter for everything, not only adding a further expense, but also reducing efficiency. We knew nothing about local policies, regulations, and cultural norms for that matter, and that would cost us a steep "learning fee" in the early stages, something we wouldn't necessarily be able to afford.

In the end, we gave up and returned to Nanning—our "plan B."

Nanning was much easier for us to wrap our heads around. Before long, we had settled on a shopping mall, which had recently added a sixth floor. Most of the stores there sold women's clothing and had been in business for long enough to have regular customers. But the sixth floor was still experiencing growing pains, so to speak: Not many people knew about it yet, and the layout was very disorganized, with stores hawking clothes for elderly women right next to those with styles more suited to teenagers. The few customers who did make their way up only left again unimpressed. This was not helped by the sky-high rents forcing businesses to close and leave in droves. Big empty spaces were not going to lure more customers up that extra flight of stairs—it was a vicious cycle. We arrived around when the first exodus was at its peak. Seeing this situation, the mall management was actively encouraging owners to lower their rents, arguing that once they had foot traffic, rental prices would naturally rise. To carry on as normal would be like killing the goose that lays the golden eggs.

The sixth floor had about 170 units, and was managed by the same company as the developers. This company, when it sold stores, made the new owners sign a ten-year property management contract, giving it control over the mall's overall operation. For us, this meant avoiding a transfer fee and securing our unit at a relatively low rent. The store became my eleventh job. Only this time, I was finally working for myself.

Since I had no savings, I borrowed twenty thousand yuan from my parents for our startup fund, while my partner contributed the same amount from his own pocket, giving us each a 50 percent share. Nanning's economy was still relatively underdeveloped back then. I remember noodles in a snail and pork broth sold for 3.5 yuan downstairs in the mall, "old friend" rice noodles for 4, and mung-bean sticky rice for 0.5.

Our first months there, the sixth floor truly had no established customer base. Anyone who came upstairs did so out of mere curiosity, with no intent to buy anything. My business partner and I assigned his wife to sourcing our products, and she selected styles based on her own taste. They were loose-fitting leisure clothes, mostly, which could already be found for sale downstairs in lots of other stores that had the advantage of proximity to the entrance and high foot traffic. There was no point in us trying to compete. Really, the higher the floor, the more suited the store to a niche market. Mainstream clothing could be bought anywhere—to do well out of it took the sort of sales volume we would not easily get. But selling niche styles also presented its challenges—the more niche something was, the more specialized, too. Neither of us being into alternative fashion ourselves, we didn't understand the subtleties that consumers cared about.

All of this only occurred to us in retrospect. We lacked business savvy. So few other stores on the sixth floor were making a profit that we weren't sure if we were the issue, or the location was. We assumed if we patiently held out until the sixth floor found its crowd, then all our worries would just go away. After a few months, we finally noticed some developments: The other store managers on the floor were all young, across the board—some were even still in school—and the customers they brought in through their social circles were of a similar age. So, their ranges catered to that demographic. Meanwhile, we were selling leisure wear that must have looked antique to all the sixteen- to twenty-four-year-old girls starting to shop next door.

Truly, the store on the other side of our wall blew up almost overnight. The boss was in her fourth year at art college and had opened the store using her boyfriend's money. She hired her cousin to watch it while she went to Guangzhou on weekends to source products. Her big break came after a feature in a Japanese fashion magazine called *ViVi* with a focus on cutesy, sweet, and foreign-influenced styles. The magazine's target readers were just the teenagers and young women that were now frequenting the sixth floor. Lena Fujii, one of the models who appeared in the magazine, was also quite popular in China. The art-college girl had been on the lookout for knockoffs of the clothing worn in the magazine for a while, and eventually, she found a supplier. She was already part of a crowd that sought to dress the way models did in magazines, so she had her regulars ready and waiting. This was an approach that even we could make sense of—stock what was in the magazines, and presto. We also happened to know her supplier, since she and my business partner's wife always traveled to Guangzhou together. We had a system in place: I stayed in the store in Nanning, and my partner, in Guangzhou, took care of collecting and shipping the goods. We didn't need to take a day and two nights each week going back and forth like other store managers.

As soon as we started selling the same clothing as her, the art-college girl freaked out. She came into our store looking for an argument and yelled at me that we were shameless for copying her. With my partner not there, she unleashed all her anger onto me. I did my best to placate her with any old nonsense. But we couldn't afford to cave just because she was angry. Sometimes business is ugly. And since we had already waded into this mire, we couldn't just return to dry land empty-handed.

A few months later, the store on the other side of us also found a supplier, and now there were three stores in a row all competing for exactly the same market.

But this was how it worked between small stores like ours that weren't brand franchises or representatives. We sourced ranges in bulk according to what was selling well. So, if one store was onto a winner, then it wouldn't be long before others who managed to find a supplier would follow suit. It was why store managers sat on their bestsellers like it was top-secret information. Talking prices with customers, we always typed them out on a calculator, in case the neighboring store workers were eavesdropping.

The business world is a place of scheming and deception. We were wary of each other, but also codependent—watching one another's stores when someone went to grab food or use the restroom, or exchanging small change when necessary. When you're stuck in a mall for a dozen hours a day, of course you are going to chat a little. You have to make the time pass somehow. So, even if there were grievances, we did our best not to argue. A fake smile when we crossed paths was usually sufficient. We just had to accept that acting two-faced was all part of the job.

Similarly, with so many people in the mall, all with too much spare time on their hands, navigating a complex web of interests, it was inevitable that gossip and rumor were rife. Some managers were more committed than others to stirring up drama, though.

It was a nightmare. I have always cared a lot about others' views of me—in the past, it's been a source of significant anxiety and frustration. Hearing others talk about me behind my back, especially when it was baseless slander, I would feel downtrodden. It brought on an overwhelming urge to prove my innocence. This work environment just became pure torment.

Fortunately, we made back our investment on the store within a year. It was money I didn't dare to sock away, though. The competition was watching us like hawks and they would swoop in the moment we paused for breath. So, to keep the store going while I went in search of a new location, I hired a young woman assistant, who I made sure earned the most of all the assistants on the sixth floor, mostly through sales commission. She received over double the rate that other stores offered, as well as tiered bonuses. While others in her position were getting at most 700 or 800 yuan, on her best month she went home with more than 2,300.

The new store location I soon chose was just around the corner on the sixth floor, right next to the main stairs, in what would have been the central area. It being so near, we couldn't sell the same clothes there as in the original store, for fear of eating into our business now that foot traffic was on a totally different level than the year before. The range we settled on was higher-quality student-style clothing from abroad—so fakes of South Korean brands like E·LAND and Teenie Weenie. Still, the quality of some knockoffs was good enough that they could almost have been mistaken for the real thing, just available to buy for only a quarter to a third of the actual price.

Because our system of work made restocking quick and easy, we opted for an approach with a low profit margin and high sales volume. When a new item became popular and quickly sold out, we could immediately buy more. Meanwhile, other stores were stuck having to wait a week or three between trips to the market, and so weren't as adaptable and couldn't risk slashing their prices as much. This also meant they didn't try to copy our goods, because we could always undercut them. If a product's sales stagnated, we had the ability to make reductions like the other stores wouldn't believe. Sitting stock only ever accumulated if not dealt with quickly, giving a store nothing but trouble.

We threw our all into this business. While other store owners opened only when it pleased them, we were willing to work hard to outpace our slowpoke competitors and put enough ground between us that they couldn't catch up. It was like in martial arts movies: Speed conquers all.

Our assistant managed the old store while I took care of the new one. Sales there had started promisingly, and with that, all my worries went away.

I have never believed in karma. Some things just seem to be fated, when really there are underlying patterns at work. That is why I should have known that, just as our new store was thriving, the seeds of trouble had already taken root.

The store diagonally opposite from the stairs changed hands shortly after we opened. The new managers were a family from Hubei—a couple and their twentysomething-year-old son, as well as his girlfriend, who showed up most days to help out. Family operations like this were unheard of on the sixth floor. The couple said they used to be in the clothing wholesale business, until the market took a downturn and they retired early. They were renting this small store to teach their son the ropes of running a business.

But they didn't make the best start. The first range of clothes they stocked didn't suit the sixth floor's style at all. I barely saw them sell a single thing. They hadn't done a full renovation of the store, only updating the sign—we had put a lot of thought into our store's look. It seemed highly unlikely they would become the tough rivals that they did. Later, I would look back and reflect that the one thing they didn't lie about was their experience in the clothing business—though whether it was wholesale or not, I couldn't say. They soon realized that my store was one of the busier ones, and after that it wasn't long before they were pulling the same stunt on us as we had on the art-college girl.

Initially, I just assumed that they were running at a loss. There were four of them working in one store, after all. But the couple were truly in it for educational purposes alone. The dad, who must have been in his fifties, would frequently shuttle back and forth to Guangzhou for restocking, while the mom, son, and girlfriend alternated watching the store. Their being indifferent about costs, we very quickly lost our edge.

The mother had a sharp tongue on her. When making sales, she had no qualms about spreading rumors to smear my store's name, claiming the clothes we sold were fakes while theirs were genuine. Since I couldn't bring myself to deal with her courteously, we became openly hostile. But this only made her more brazen with her gossip, creating no end of problems for us. It was hellish.

Plenty of other incidents went down over this time. My business partner—who would come to Nanning every month for a few days to see how the mall was changing—got into a fight with another store owner. Our relationship with the other sixth-floor store had always been unfriendly, but after the scuffle, the store owner refused to give in and called three thugs for backup. They arrived with vegetable knives hidden on their person and tried to drag my partner out of the mall. But mall security had already alerted the cops, who swooped in, and the three thugs made off while they still could. My partner and the other guy were not so lucky, and were taken into custody. At the station, they were reprimanded and made to write statements. The police told them that if they didn't leave each other be, the punishment would be much more severe the next time. After they were both carried off, I went straight to repair relations with the storekeeper's girlfriend and, that evening, the four of us all ate a meal of baked tilapia together on Longsheng Street. Food as peace offering. It would be no good for us to go on as we had been with the cops now keeping an eye on things. But I'm not exaggerating when I say they were involved with local thugs. I had heard multiple times that the girlfriend's parents were the heads of some cell phone stealing gang. Everybody knew this, but nobody seemed to think it was a big deal. No one said anything bad about them behind their backs. It was as if running a women's clothing store and organized cell phone theft were just alternative career paths. Wanting to be prepared for anything, I took a vegetable knife of my own to our peacemaking meal, wrapped in newspaper and stuck in my pants waist, covered by layers of clothing. As long as our two stores remained in competition, the animosity wouldn't disappear so easily. Any so-called reconciliation was just outward talk. Business disputes happened all the time in the mall, almost every day, they just rarely escalated to the point where police became involved.

Another thing that happened was my girlfriend broke up with me. Her mom had been nagging at her to go abroad, and she had dithered on my account. This had put me on the receiving end of a lot of her negative emotions—she was constantly frustrated that I was falling short of her expectations. I had, in fact, subtly hinted that I would respect her decision and support her, no matter what. But I didn't dare to suggest a split myself, in case she accused me of being unambitious and irresponsible—so, a failure. And maybe people would say she was right. But our relationship had taken its toll on my mental state. At my worst, I had felt on the verge of depression. That's why, when she made her mind up to go, I didn't feel sad, but relieved. I knew very well that I wouldn't be able to give her what she wanted.

She has long since settled down in another country, where she leads a positive, fulfilling life. It is clear she made the right decision—we have managed to stay amicable all these years, rather than tearing each other apart. But back then, alongside the relief, I also found myself enveloped by this strange sense of aimlessness. For so long, she had been my primary motivation to work hard and build the business, and now that this "burden" was gone, I felt like my energy had vanished along with it.

I stayed in Nanning for two-plus years altogether. After we got our business on track a few months in, there was a long stretch of time where I lived my whole life between point A and point B: waking up and heading straight to the mall, then going back to my place at 10 P.M. My only days off all year were for the Spring Festival. It was only when I left the city that I realized I had hardly seen any of it beyond the mall. There were entire districts I'd never even heard of. My mind was consumed by the mall and the business. I had no idea what was happening in the outside world, nor did I care. Even the Beijing Olympics passed me by unnoticed. The only thing that momentarily snapped me out of it was the Wenchuan earthquake. The tremors reached the mall, causing the building to sway. Property management quickly evacuated everyone, and we all gathered outside. This is the only "news event" that left any impression from all that time.

The mall shut for a few days over the Spring Festival in 2009. On the afternoon of Lunar New Year's Eve, many of the storekeepers went home early. Our assistant had left the day before. I was the last one out of the mall. I had bought an evening train ticket and had a window of free time before departure. It was drizzling outside, the ground was slick with water, and the usually busy main street was empty. Somewhere beyond the closed storefronts, there were firecrackers going off in the distance. I ate dinner at the only McDonalds with the lights still on, then walked to the train station. The feeling that came over me as I made my way through the deserted streets was one of utter hopelessness. I try to avoid such self-pitying thoughts today—I live in a time of peace and have never really, truly suffered, so it's melodramatic to talk like that. But I vividly remember that afternoon—or maybe the afternoon etched itself into my memory through sheer force of feeling: It occurred to me that being born into this world isn't necessarily a blessing.

We hadn't signed a lease directly with the owner for our new location, but were subletting from the previous storekeeper. We had our doubts we could make it work at the start. When we had to find a different fashion direction from the first store, we worried about repeating our earlier mistakes. By subletting, we avoided having to pay a transfer fee to the previous tenant, who just so happened to be the younger sister of the owner. The surrounding storekeepers all told us she was a playful woman with very little interest in running the place, which her older sister initially let her use in the hope it would help her settle down. But then she became pregnant and wanted to take a step back. After some discussion, my partner and I decided we were better off paying a slightly higher rent to her every month than swallowing the transfer fee and binding ourselves with a more official contract, which would leave us less margin for errors. But the lack of a contract with the owner was also the downside—the younger sister might decide at any moment she wanted the space back, or a problem might arise in their agreement and we would be impacted. Their being sisters, though, we were fairly confident their lease would be secure and neither of them would go back on their word all of a sudden. With a baby on the way, the younger sister would be giving even more of her time to family and unlikely to change her mind about a business she wasn't all that committed to in the first place. So, I gave it a shot, and we negotiated a sublease with her. But sometimes, when times get hard, even a sip of cold water can catch in the throat.

It was a year later when she contacted me saying she wanted to take the store back. I was baffled. Everything I had heard suggested she had no ambition for the business—there used to be days on end when she wouldn't show up at the store. Besides, her child was not even a year old yet; what was she thinking going back to selling clothing? If this was a ploy to raise the rent, she could have just spoken with me directly. Eventually, I started to suspect someone else had put her up to it—like the thug my business partner fought with. I had no choice but to negotiate with her. In the end, all I managed to secure was a three-month extension.

By that point, I was already seeing signs of social anxiety in myself. The excitement I used to feel whenever a customer entered had been replaced by dread and irritation. I avoided conversations if I could, other than with people I knew and trusted. When strangers smiled at me, I would think there was malice in it. If I argued with someone about anything, even if I had no reason to be angry, I was left shivering uncontrollably—I don't know if this is what people mean by "shaking with rage," but I had never experienced anything like it before.

After my partner and I lost our second store, I decided to call it a day. I didn't want to stay in business. We parted ways, amicably, with no loose ends to tie up. After I left Nanning, he brought in a new business partner, who was a relative of his wife. He would go on to run four stores at his high point, but he's changed industry now. Meanwhile, I went home and held off on finding new work. Nothing I could have secured would have been even slightly better, but this wasn't the reason. I had spent every day of the past two years confined to a closed, windowless space, surrounded by smiling yet conniving competitors and constantly bombarded with gossip and slander. I had never badmouthed anyone behind their back, but I had acted aggressively in the name of business—finding ways to outmaneuver and squeeze out the competition. There were only so many customers who visited the mall in a day, and if they shopped in my store, they wouldn't then buy from someone else's. There were times I felt guilty—like with the art-college girl. But more often than not, I felt bitter and resentful. When I finally walked away from the mall business and stepped back into the open air, I experienced a strange aversion to light. I had been away from the sun for far too long. In Nanning, the only time I spent outside each day was the fifteen minutes it took to walk to work.

I became fearful of people, paranoid and suspicious. I often felt like passersby in the street were giving me strange looks. But when I got home and looked in the mirror, scrutinized my appearance, I couldn't find anything unusual. Sometimes I would glare back at them, only to realize their expression was perfectly natural. Some of them weren't even looking at me.

I stopped answering calls from unknown numbers, and sometimes ignored those from people I knew. I stopped replying in my old classmates' group chat and skipped any gatherings. One classmate called me repeatedly, but I never picked up. For years, I lost touch with all of them except the classmate I had gone into business with. (This was as much to do with a feeling I had fallen behind as with my mental state—a feeling I wasn't as good as them. It took me years to overcome that misplaced sense of inferiority.) Even when friends messaged on QQ (this was before the days of WeChat), I would agonize for ages before responding. I worried that what I wrote would fall short in some way—that the tone would be off, or the wording—even if their message had been casual. The more I valued someone, the more self-conscious and anxious I became interacting with them, whereas I found I could relax around acquaintances I didn't care about all that much. It was ironic.

Writing

I was walking by the roadside once, when an illegal taxi bike cut across the street at a red light up ahead and made a quick U-turn into traffic, grazing me as it passed and catching me completely off guard. The driver slammed on the brakes. I wasn't hurt thankfully, just shaken up. Raging, I started to yell at the driver, and even cuffed him on the shoulder, which was when a crowd formed around us and began blasting me for giving the cabbie a hard time.

Cabdrivers have a tough enough time of it already, the crowd argued, working rain or shine to scrape by, without me adding to their troubles. I should show them some sympathy. Which I agreed with, but I replied, "What if I had been a pregnant woman that he hit?" To which the crowd said nothing. Instead, seeing I wasn't backing down, a young man stepped forward. "So you like to fight?" he said. "I'll fight you." But before he had a chance to escalate, the older men and women dragged him away. The message our seniors hoped to impart: Peace is precious; leave people to go their own ways, unmolested. But I never planned to punish the guy, I just likely had some serious anger that needed venting. Also, who was to say the cabbie earned any less than I did, or that his work was more tiring than mine?

This is the one time in my life I've gone against a group in public and stood up to people's criticisms. It is a mark of the latent hysteria I was experiencing in that period, my nerves stretched taut right below the surface, ready to snap. Although not entirely a result of this interaction, it was about from then onward that I would shut myself away in my room every day and rarely venture outside.

After leaving my business partner, I returned my parents' twenty thousand yuan and lived on the few dozen thousand that left me. My parents didn't know what I'd been through and still don't know to this day. They only saw that I had stopped working, stopped going out and meeting people, and it worried them, but they had no idea how to help. They're kindhearted, sensible people who struggled to understand that, sometimes, society doesn't make sense. But I wasn't doing nothing with all that time spent alone in my room—I had started trying to write. This was October 2009.

Running a business is time-consuming. But in the mall, it usually wasn't until two or three in the afternoon that customers would start to trickle in, and I often had the mornings to myself. I would read in the store to pass the long hours. Most books I chose for pure entertainment value, but I picked up some literary works, as well. I could count on my fingers how many. There was *The Catcher in the Rye*, which I found moving. Salinger's *Nine Stories* and *Raise High the Roof Beam, Carpenters and Seymour* had some great stories. All of them were seemingly about how purity and truth are incompatible with this world, to the extent they are destroyed. My earliest writings were just pale imitations of Salinger's.

Then, I read Raymond Carver. The collapse of everyday lives he describes affected me very deeply. And Richard Yates—he was incredibly gentle, and very melancholy in a way that captivated me far more back then than it does now. Also, Truman Capote, whose semi-autobiographical children's stories I found to be very touching and much better than *Breakfast at Tiffany's*.

I was just fascinated by American realism; the lives and emotions described in these stories were powerfully resonant. This might have been to do with the fact that commodity society and consumerism were taking over the entire world: People's life experiences were being universally homogenized.

The more literary works I read, the more distant I felt from my reality. My life had been plagued by setbacks and adversity, whether in my work, or business, or my emotional state. I sought approval within a system of values that didn't suit me, and was constantly disappointed and knocked back. I'm not putting the whole blame for my failures on my environment. I just wish I'd known that I didn't need the acceptance of others. I ought to have been doing what I enjoy doing and am good at, like writing. Clearly, the real world seemed so barren to me then that the world of the mind had become my greener pastures.

I read Ernest Hemingway next. His subjects were as far removed from my reality as could be. He was also very unlike me as a person—even opposite me, in certain regards. It was he who came up with the "iceberg theory"—he believed that a big part of what makes an iceberg so impressive is that only one-eighth of it is above water, with the rest left for us to conjure up with our imagination. In writing, the eighth visible on the surface is the words and images, while the submerged, greater portion comprises the thought and emotion. The former is what the author puts down with their pen; the latter is contained within. This was a significant lesson for me to learn early on in my writing experiments. The unwritten part is where the enormity and weight of a story should reside; and the art of story writing is in expressing with as few words and images as possible limitless thought and feeling.

This is what I spent my time practicing, whenever I put pen to paper: how to leave empty space and silence, and knowing what not to write. But as I read more widely, I came to realize that the iceberg theory is not a singular truth—art can break all the rules. Still, it was a very sharp blade.

I wrote a series of stories based on my own experiences, with characters and plots almost entirely drawn from real prototypes, and posted them in a literary forum online. Shortly after, a few pieces were printed in literary journals, for meager pay. One story of eight thousand words didn't earn me even three hundred yuan. I remember because it was the lowest rate I ever received. I had once, briefly, fantasized about making a living as a writer, but this quickly shattered any delusions.

The experiences I'm sharing in this chapter were the basis for most of those stories. It would be amusing now to read them side by side with the newer accounts. Those stories come across as serious and stiff, moralistic and self-pitying, while my more recent work is much easier going—both for the reader and for myself when doing the writing. This book required none of the effort of invention, I just put down things as they were. Cooking up stories out of thin air is not a skill I have ever had, especially when it comes to plot. There is a lot in this book that I left out of the fiction—the seven-eighths I had decided were to stay underwater. Here, every choice I made over those years is laid bare—the lead-up, the motive—and I examine my feelings and mental state myself, and give more context about the settings and environments. I won't try to claim that everything you're reading is one hundred percent objective, though, because there is no such thing when it comes to writing. Subjectivity in our perspectives and standpoints is inevitable; it's why the same incident will always vary between different accounts. I can only endeavor to respect the facts and be unbiased wherever possible. Bear in mind, there might have been motivating forces acting on my psychology that even I wasn't aware of. I can hardly recall the major reason I chose a course of action in some cases, since this all happened so long ago now.

But I digress. This stretch of writing activity continued over two years, and though it wasn't a job per se, I invested more care and commitment into it than I had into all my jobs put together.

From day one of my writing practice, I fostered a habit of keeping a journal, noting down snatches of thoughts, feelings, and insights as they came to me. After flicking back through the entries from those years, I want to pick out two, in particular. The first encapsulates the spirit of my time spent roaming in Beijing and creating. It's a period I look back on fondly, which played a big role in my living for myself and doing what I wanted to do. I made plenty of mistakes, of course, and hurt people, but the boundless ambition we as a group of friends shared, for authenticity and disciplined growth, still stands today as the most formative revelation in my life, the first beam of light that ever lit my way. Sometimes this ambition took the form of self-interest, mulishness, or cruelty, but; recognizing this and taming those impulses was all part of the journey.

The second entry is a record of the negative feelings I harbored toward work at some moment in the past. Years old now, both passages seem exaggerated and childish today, but they are still paths my mind once wandered, which can explain, directly or indirectly, the shift I would later experience in my attitude toward work.

The first is titled "Rock as Art" and is about rock music. But I think if I was writing it now, I would call it "Do Not Go Gentle into That Good Night":

A. A distinctive characteristic of "rock as art form" is that its formal success depends heavily and directly on the artist having a unique spirit and personality.

B. Rock's charm comes from the synergy between artist and music: the artist's soul (the content) and the music (the form) in alignment.

C. Rock musicians (artists) search their whole lives for the sound that chimes with their very being.

D. It is why true rock musicians are intolerant of craftiness, and repelled by music that is elegant, refined, and skillful but lacks soul.

E. Rock rails against hypocrisy, numbness, mediocrity, order, and dogma, and is itself willful, brutal, extreme, confused, and despairing. Its power lies in destruction rather than construction.

F. Rock often rebels against the "healthy" world through "unhealthy" means.

G. The best rock isn't necessarily the most moving song, most beautiful voice, or virtuoso performance; it's about the opposite extreme: loathing good technique, practice, and neatness, and relishing the simple, the impulsive, and the rough around the edges.

H. "Bias" is often more creative and expressive. Art does not reject "bias," because it is not driven by opinions or advocacy, it only cares whether the "bias" is unique and insightful. Rock takes the same approach.

I. Besides, there is no such thing as impartiality; there is only bias.

J. Songwriting is creation, as is performing; performance is the art form of presentation.

K. Since rock is performance art, interpretation is accepted as long as it is sincere. Trying to express generosity, emotions, or attitudes in creation that one doesn't genuinely possess is a betrayal of the spirit of rock.

L. At the core of the spirit of rock is authenticity.

M. The soul of a rock band is often the most standout personality.

N. People say rock music is not a genre but a mindset. What they mean is rock is a formal expression of life and the individual through art, and not an exploration of musical form. This is why rock is often dismissed as "primitive."

O. Rock artists focus on exploring human nature and refining perceptions, right down to interrogating the soul. They delve deeper, enrich and shape themselves; see their growth as people as the greatest, if not the only, guarantee of artistic accomplishment.

P. Although this self-refinement is inevitably reflected in their oeuvre and performances, alongside their experiments in musical form, the work on themselves comes first—the one must follow the other.

Q. Already extraordinary individuals from the start, rock musicians dedicate themselves to becoming ever more sensitive and radical—it is a natural instinct they have for sustaining their artistic vitality and originality. They seek unique expressions for even the most insignificant parts of themselves, until, ultimately, the intensity of the love and hate they feel grows to such an unbearable degree that it leads to mental breakdown, or at least brings them to the brink of one. This is often not a conscious choice, but a spontaneous act of spirit.

R. Rock idolizes and feeds on self-destructive heroes.

S. It is a road of no return: When they choose—or are forced—to put down their instruments, their artistic life comes to an end. "Dead" rock artists still can write songs and perform, but it's different.

T. Rock, more than any other art form, requires self-sacrifice. This is something the artist does not get to decide. A lot of "dead" rock musicians are still with us.

U. But excessive dramatization and interpretation of the self is a trap that average folk often fail to recognize. True rock artists are geniuses, and they are fully aware of this fact.

V. In other words, rock is the geniuses' art.

W. Like Faust, rock singers trade their soul with the devil; with brilliance comes loneliness, conflict, pain, and exhaustion. True rock music, even if it sounds cheerful or energetic on the surface, is the artist crying out as they descend into the abyss.

The second passage is about work and is untitled:

Work for the sole purpose of making a living is a miserable prison, which is why very few people will confess that this is what they do. The common claims go: I find my job interesting, I like my colleagues, work makes me feel fulfilled. Such statements, even when true, are still one-sided—there are ways outside of work to do what interests us, spend time with people we like, and lead fulfilling lives. The older generation are generally more forthright. They will ask how you are going to look after yourself if you don't work. They don't consider shackling oneself with a job, limiting one's freedoms, to be a sorry thing at all. Blind toil brings honor, they say. Indeed, in their day, we had no artists or philosophers, so the only people who didn't work were the indolent.

Maugham wrote that not every man, whose food and warmth are supplied, knows what to do with themself once the business of the workday is done. It was a grim, even cruel, time that left us so pitifully stunted and small-minded, meanwhile society has long since changed. Consumerism is the new ideology, a different kind of lifelong imprisonment, which only gives the appearance of freedom. Compared with restricting you from doing everything you want, it is certainly the more stable and lasting way to maintain social order—instilling in you a sense of what you need and providing the means to achieve it. But this is still a form of enslavement, one in which the individual's main route to self-realization remains through work. So, we attach importance to not only our own work but other people's. Work is already our chief mark of identity. Old classmates reuniting after a long time will first ask each other what they do nowadays. Strangers who meet on a train learn about each other's jobs before their hobbies and interests. Some people seem suited to finding their success and happiness through work—I'm referring to the jobs that most people recognize as having material returns. But they are far from the majority. Work is a means of survival, not the meaning of life. It is only now, thanks to society's advancements, that unlike our distant ancestors we can work ourselves to the bone without freezing or starving to death. We no longer need to spend five sleepless days and nights tracking a wooly mammoth, in the hope of felling it before we are utterly spent, then drag its bloody flesh for dozens of miles by foot back to our dank caves, to feed our fur-covered women and children. If most of us woke up to find ourselves in that situation, we would likely choose the quickest way out. Fortunately, we have complex social structures and production methods that make our work efficient and dignified, and so seemingly unlike those gory hunts—even when, at their core, they are just the same.

My Twelfth Job

I seem to remember I had stayed indoors for almost two years when I finally felt like going outside again and stretching my legs. I was experiencing writer's block, and it was becoming time I shored up my savings, which despite my living with my parents were down to half on account of my book-buying habit. I didn't feel ready to return to work: The prospect of having to interact with people was intimidating. But an old colleague, one of the other graphic designers from the anime magazine, reached out. He had always been genial, with an easy laugh, and we got along well. He had gone into business himself and done much better than I had. The store he had opened in a mall on Shangxiajiu Street was now one of six. We met up to reminisce about old times and spent much of the day happily chatting. He told me that brick-and-mortar stores were becoming harder and harder to run, and that everything was moving online.

This was midway through 2011. He had just rented a six-thousand-square-foot warehouse, with the plan to make a serious go of an online store, while phasing out the existing operations. Knowing I had experience selling women's clothing and was out of work, he encouraged me to open an online store of my own. I was unable to pay for a large warehouse like his, so he suggested I rent a room near the wholesale market. This way, I could just wait until someone made an order, go around the corner, and pick up what was purchased, and I didn't need many funds to get the business off the ground. So I followed his advice—it would be my twelfth job.

I realized very quickly that the business was never going to bring in any money, but if I could keep my costs low I might just about break even.

I just wasn't fully invested in the store—I had too much reading and writing I wanted to do. I thought I could juggle the two things at once, but the reality was I ended up doing a sub-par job of both. Taobao was nowhere near as competitive as it is now—online traders would later look back at those years as the golden era of the platform. There was money to be made whatever you did, but I was too indifferent to make even that work, which shows just how unsuited I am to business. Part of the problem was I had to leave my rented room occasionally, where I spent most of my time, so I could talk with wholesalers and couriers, and collect and mail goods. My interactions with them were disastrous.

I was too embarrassed to look most of the sellers in the eye, worried what they would think about me only buying a few items at a time. Plenty of other people did this, so I was doing nothing wrong, but my sense of shame and fear was overwhelming. This was even with me making bigger purchases when I could, as amends. If a style was selling well, I would stock up on it in an effort to save face, as well as reduce how often I had to return and suffer through another conversation with a storekeeper.

My wish was that I could be see-through—devoid of presence, invisible to everyone. But it was not to be. I must have stood out in some way from the other regular buyers, because one storekeeper in particular took note of the diffident, polite man who always asked how she was, said thank you when he left, and never stuck around to chat or expected anything more. She sold a T-shirt I kept in my store for a long time, at what I thought was an agreed-upon price since the wholesalers rarely welcomed bargaining. Then one day I went to restock, and she told me the price was two yuan lower. In that moment, it dawned on me why she had looked like she wanted to say something the last few visits. The price must have dropped some time earlier, and she had thought it strange to tell me if I wasn't going to ask—why give up the extra profit if I was happy to pay the old price?

Back at my store in Nanning, although I had never fetched the product myself, I still knew the buying price of every item we sold. Some styles that were expensive when they first arrived on the market would drop in price as the merchant expanded their production and per-item costs decreased. Plus, counterfeiting drove prices down, so it was nothing unusual that this happened. Experienced buyers simply made sure to confirm the price with the supplier every time they restocked. But I didn't check it once, after that first time, for a litany of reasons: I lacked experience, I bought too little, I felt embarrassed, and, of course, it would mean engaging in conversation. All of this amounted to wanting the ground to swallow me up. I didn't trade with her again, after that. I felt like too much of an idiot to show my face ever again.

I also have stories that involve the delivery guys. At the time, the best of the Big Five were YTO, then ZTO Express. The worst was HT Express (which is, ironically, now BEST Express). That was the courier I used, because it generally offered lower fees for smaller clients. But the guy they sent was not even twenty years old. I found it hard to talk business with him. He was still a child, and an unpunctual child at that. It was no good trying to arrange a pickup. He wouldn't answer when I asked what time he was going to be free. And he refused to come upstairs to collect parcels. He would call me in advance and make me wait downstairs, sometimes for ages.

I could forgive him all this—I couldn't blame him, really—if only he had been better at telling me when he wasn't going to make it. Sometimes, I wouldn't get a message until the night: too busy, will come tomorrow. This meant orders reached customers a day late. People were newer to online shopping back then and could be quick to worry, nudging me to send off their items just hours after they had paid. So, I kept vigil by my cell phone for whole evenings, waiting for his call, in case I started on something else and missed it, but also too cowardly to call him myself and get him to hurry up. When he never showed, my anxiety would skyrocket. Eventually, it started to give me stomachaches.

Then, another courier stepped in when the younger guy took a day off. This new courier didn't make me wait downstairs for him, but came up himself to collect the parcel. When I paid, he frowned. "You always pay this much?" he asked.

The young guy had said the rate was eight yuan, I replied.

"Shit, that kid!" the new courier swore.

I understood right away. The depot didn't charge eight yuan. The kid was pocketing some. I had been working with him for the better part of a year—a whole lot of time where I could have spoken with his boss or negotiated on price. The money I would have saved! I had been played by a child. I felt furious, and pathetic. I didn't want to see him again.

I switched to using ZTO Express the very next day. The boss from the HT Express depot was a subcontractor—I had never met her, but she called me. Not to ask why I had stopped using their services, because I'm sure she knew. She just tactfully inquired about the price ZTO Express had given me. It was also eight yuan, but I didn't tell her that.

In my writing at this point, I was starting to look back at the realist stories I had written earlier as outdated and cliché. I entered a period of "metamorphosis," shamefaced at reading my own writing. The literary forum I was part of only exacerbated this inferiority complex, despite also giving me a lot of very helpful inspiration. The authors I had liked two years earlier were now old hat to me. Having gone through their work with a fine-tooth comb, reading some maybe ten-plus times, I had grown tired of it. I began venturing into "modernism"—I was being practical about aesthetics, really, but I didn't know this at the time.

Soon, I had exchanged my muse Salinger for Kafka. In one reply on the forum, I wrote, "I no longer like Carver, he's too popular, too easy to get, his style has been reduced to a formula."

I replaced him with Joyce, even though I had only read *Dubliners*. *Ulysses* would come later. But nobody picked up that he was who I was imitating, so I never mentioned his name.

I was slowly starting to notice I had developed a malicious streak. As a guest moderator for the forum, part of my role was to read every piece that users posted on the stories page and comment on as many of them as I could. In cases where a story didn't do anything for me, I left inappropriate comments, most of them negative. It didn't occur to me I was being spiteful. I honestly believed this was what constructive feedback looked like, and I was doing people a favor by sharing with them everything I thought of their work. Discussion on the forum tended to be pointed, anyway. People did not mince their words. In fact, more than appropriateness, or a lack thereof, they were concerned by suck-ups and cliques. I'm sure I hurt some people acting like I did—I should have kept my mouth shut. The aggression was a defense mechanism that stemmed from my own insecurities. This was a disappointing realization to have. It made me doubt myself and my writing further.

I chose to take a break from the internet for a while. I had spent too much time online in the past year, managing the store and fulfilling my moderator duties. I had fallen out of touch with reality. I needed to rediscover nature, or get away from society, one or the other. This was part of what pushed me to move to Yunnan.

Another factor was that my account had stagnated. My income from the store was just about covering my rent and meals. Already, I lived very frugally. I kept the store open for a year or so, changing apartments once in the middle when I changed wholesale markets. But my motivation only ever dwindled, while my desperation to never have to talk with merchants, couriers, and my landlord again grew. My writing had also come to a standstill: I wanted to erase everything I'd done before, but Kafka, as Joyce, isn't an easy man to emulate, especially when your attention is divided.

Ultimately, there came a day when I decided that was it: the business was going nowhere, I was hard up, I was being unkind online; my mental health was in shambles, my mindset beginning to warp. It was time for a change of environment, not from one side of the city to the other, but to a new place entirely.

One of my Beijing friends, who I was back in contact with, was a children's book illustrator, self-employed, and could live anywhere. After some discussion, we settled on Yunnan. Another friend had recently recommended Dali to us, in the northwest of the province, saying he planned to move there himself, so the two of us decided we would give it a try. In the end, he never joined us.

My Thirteenth and Fourteenth Jobs

My friend and I each moved into our own rental apartments in Xiaguan, Dali, in September 2012. He continued doing illustration, while I started looking for work. My apartment included two bedrooms, a toilet, and a hallway, with no living room. Rent was a thousand yuan for three months. I chose not to install internet, to force myself to go online less. I was disappointed in my previous behavior. I had also stopped writing. I felt like I had nothing to say. Still, I kept up my journal. The passage about rock as art came from this time. I had bought my first smartphone before leaving for Yunnan, a secondhand Huawei with a crude Android system and a screen resolution of only 320x240. This was where I did my writing from then on, until 2020 when I changed back to using my laptop.

My thirteenth job was in property management at a mall in Xiaguan, which is just another way of saying that I was a security guard. We were responsible for only the first, second, and third floors. The supermarket, furniture and home store, and residences, from the fourth floor up, were outside our jurisdiction. We worked in four teams of four, in a three-shift system, so there were guards on duty around the clock. It was the same arrangement as when I had been at the gas station, only I earned 300 yuan less than the 1,800 a month I'd been on back then. In other words, twelve years had passed, and with the same workload as before, my pay was somehow still lower, which tells you how underdeveloped Xiaguan was. But this is partly what drew me there. At the fourth-floor supermarket, I could get a quick meal for 4 yuan; a bowl of pulled pork and rice noodles cost

5 yuan in the street; our rent was 330 yuan per month. I could quite happily live on 1,500 yuan.

Xiaguan stood at the southern end of Erhai Lake, by the mouth of the Xi'er River. The views were beautiful in this urban area beside the water, with green hills visible to the west. The locals I worked with liked to say, "Our Xiaguan is the luckiest place to be!" They wore such pride on their faces, as if it was the honor of their lives to live there. But, in their dialect, the word that sounded to me like "lucky"—"*haozai*"—actually meant something more like "livable."

The job itself was very relaxed. It was the sort of work I would have said only older folk did, and that would have suited me just fine had it turned out to be true—working alongside seniors was preferable, really. But many of my colleagues were closer in age to myself. One guy was barely twenty. I knew full well there were no prospects in this line of work, but I wasn't there to think about the future. I wanted to live, as much as possible, in the present. I suspected my mediocrity as a writer was a symptom of my mediocre existence, and I was eager for a new lease on life.

Our security control room was little more than a poky cabin of aluminum composite panels and glass, hidden away behind the main building, along with the bike shed. Part of our job was to keep an eye on the bicycles, electric bikes, and motorbikes parked there, which meant one of the team had to stay in the control room at all times. Patrolling the mall interior—the rest of the job—was tedious work. Walking as slowly as possible, it still took one of us less than half an hour to cover all three floors. Yet, there were three of us assigned to the task.

The mall was also dead most of the time, so with nothing else to do, the store assistants would watch me shuffle past on my rounds. Some of my colleagues liked to stop and talk with them, but I never did. Outside the main mall door was a parking lot that was handled by subcontractors and so wasn't really ours to worry about. But I still headed out there occasionally, scanning the area like I was checking on the cars' safety. Really, I was just fed up and wanted some fresh air.

On the day shift, we took turns sitting in the control room, which was equally boring, but at least there were newspapers to browse. I preferred the night shift, because instead of catching up on the news, we could nap. Our boss was perfectly happy to turn a blind eye. Xiaguan was just that peaceful. Even the local organized gangs had enough ambition to light out for more prosperous lands.

One evening, we had a barbecue in the control room. I could tell it wasn't the first time this had happened, and I knew we weren't supposed to, but I didn't feel worried. I was happy to go along with it. What surprised me was they used a portable electric heater to cook the food. The heater looked somewhat like an anti-mosquito lamp, just much larger, and instead of emitting UV light, the tubes inside were infrared. Fitted over these, for protection, was a metal grate. My colleagues laid the heater on its side, and the food on the grate to cook. Hot coals would have done the job much more quickly, but we had the whole night ahead of us. The electric heater normally sat down by everyone's feet, where it had long become dusty and dirty, but nobody minded, so I didn't either. We each pitched in twenty yuan, and a colleague rode their electric bike to the nearby barbecue stall to buy marinated ingredients. He also brought back a bottle of Snow Mountain buckwheat liquor. For some reason, everybody was under the impression I wouldn't dare to drink while on shift. They must have considered me a rule follower. But I truly wasn't worried! They were drinking, so why shouldn't I. After I took my first sip, they all gave me a thumbs-up.

Life in Xiaguan was good. Although I wasn't making all that much, I never had to work more than eight hours a day. The job also fell well within my capabilities, which was a relief. Everyone there treated me really nicely, sometimes to the extent I felt like a foreign guest. Maybe this was because I was the only employee from outside the province.

My social anxiety just wasn't a thing with my colleagues. They knew very little about my past, and I very little about theirs, and no one had any interest in prying. They were pure of heart, straightforward people, that was how it seemed to me. Probably, their salaries made it pointless for them to try to be anything more. No one had plans to get ahead, anyone who did had likely left for more developed areas. The climate also suited me just right: The winter was warm, the summer cool, the sunlight plentiful, and the wind and rain didn't mess around. It was like the gods smiled on Xiaguan. After two months of being a security guard, I was so much more relaxed, I felt like a different person. It was a big improvement.

Then, the HR manager called me into her office one day to recommend an apprenticeship at the fourth-floor bakery. It paid the same as being a guard, but the job was better. "You won't learn any new skills as a security guard," she told me.

I wasn't keen on leaving my colleagues and newfound friends, but I accepted her goodwill without hesitation, even if only to avoid disappointing her. It just so happened that the owner of the bakery was the mall manager's daughter, and HR handled staffing for both. The other guards were all very supportive of the move, saying it was a waste for me to stay in security. They did warn me, though, "You better remember to bring us pastries down to eat." They were joking, but I didn't forget.

The bakery's kitchen included a bread and pastries section and a cake section, each with its own production room (which we called the shaping rooms) and a baking room. The bread section also had rooms for proofing and kneading and a small workspace for making puff pastry and croissants. There was also a communal ingredients room.

I was assigned to the bread section. The only chef there, when I started, was the cake chef, the baker having just left. It was a month or so before the boss hired another. In the bread section, there were two sous-chefs (one of whom was new) and six apprentices (one of whom was me). It quickly became apparent that I was the second oldest in our section, with even the sous-chefs being younger than me. Besides myself and one other Han person, the eight-person team was made up of members of the local ethnic groups: three Bai, two Hui, and one Dai.

As the newest arrival, I was given various odd jobs to do, portioning the dough and ingredients, kneading, mixing, and restocking. I also helped with the lower-skill products like egg tarts, puff pastry, and cookies, but I was rarely allowed near the bread when it came to shaping, as my few attempts all came out looking totally different. One of the sous-chefs was in charge of making the dough and shaping, and the other responsible for the puff pastry, croissants, baguettes, and toasted sandwiches. Of course, when it got busy, the division of labor wasn't so clear-cut—even I might be asked to shape some bread, in the full knowledge the loaves were going to be very inconsistent. The new head chef that joined a month into my time there was from Chongqing. He had left baking behind once already, to become a flour salesman, and it had been this that brought him to our bakery originally. But our boss had talked him into staying on as head baker. Basically, finding a skilled baker in Xiaguan was not easy. This new head chef made some adjustments to work arrangements, and I was assigned to the bread section's baking room.

Before the proofed bread went into the oven, there were often still final touches to make: more shaping, an egg or an oil wash, seasoning. And once the bread was out of the oven, there was buttercream, icing sugar, fruit, and decoration to add. In the baking room, as well as the large, triple-deck commercial oven, there was a convection oven for the egg tarts, puff pastry, and cookies, an electric basket fryer for donuts, and a proofing cabinet with preset time, temperature, and humidity functions. At the end of every day, we loaded it up with that afternoon's shaped doughs so they would be ready for baking first thing the next morning.

The baking-room staff started and ended their day an hour earlier than the shaping-room staff, and arrived two hours earlier than when the bakery opened, so we were always the first there, at maybe 7 A.M. Xiaguan was on the same time as Beijing, even though it is in a different time zone, UTC+07:00, so the days got light late. When I arrived at the bakery in winter, the sky was still dark.

Our fresh products could only be kept for a day. Any we didn't manage to sell were supposed to be disposed of the following morning. Instead, when we arrived at the bakery, bright and early, we started work by eating all of the leftovers from the day before, to save on breakfast costs. Occasionally, our arrival would send mice scurrying out of the piles of bread we had left on the countertops after removing them from the display cabinets. But nobody seemed to mind much, as long as we checked the individual pieces for nibble marks before tucking in ourselves. It was an impossibility to get rid of all the mice, everybody in the mall's food services knew that, so we just became numb to them. We shared a floor with the supermarket and supermarket storehouse. It was like paradise for the mice, with all the hiding places and food everywhere, and they had free rein. That's not to say we didn't try to kill them—the sticky traps were the most effective method we found, and we basically caught something every evening. But more always came. It makes you despair—that over intelligence and agility, reproductive power is the true superior trait.

The boss never said anything about us eating out-of-date bread every day, even though she almost certainly knew we were doing it. But from her perspective, it was much more economical to cover our breakfasts than to give everyone a raise. Plus, if she never acknowledged it, the fault remained ours if we ever got sick.

As an apprentice, I naturally learned a lot that was new to me. But the bakery wasn't really a school, so nobody had any duty to teach me anything. The pastry chef told us he started work in a cake shop at seventeen, and for the first three years, the chef only let him bake the bases of the cakes. He learned nothing, he said. But the idea was to instill discipline in us, and get us used to doing as we were told without worrying about the craft, because that's not something that can be mastered overnight. His focus was on researching and developing new products, sourcing ingredients, allocating tasks, and doing quality control. Rarely did he give direct training or supervision. Usually, that fell to the two sous-chefs, although they weren't keen on passing on their skills either—partly because they were already very busy, but also, they had in the back of their minds the concern that "teaching the disciple might starve the master." As soon as personal interests are involved, relationships between people become much more complicated. Both the sous-chefs were very careful about how they answered our questions, purposefully giving only the bare minimum of details, never more than we absolutely needed to know. By contrast, my security guard colleagues hadn't hesitated to show me how the escalator worked. Since there was zero skill involved, they didn't risk being replaced by me once I knew how to do their job. But making bread was a skill with value. A beginners' course alone could cost several thousand yuan to join. The sous-chefs had worked hard to acquire these techniques, gone through trials and tribulations to get where they were. So, my questions and requests for demonstrations were often met with a frown like they had suddenly partially lost their capacity for speech and were racking their brains for the right words. When they would finally open their mouths, all that came out was, "Go ask so-and-so. I showed them, already."

So-and-so would be my fellow apprentice, who started a few days earlier, but was still stuck alongside me at the bottom rung of the workplace hierarchy. So-and-so should have known my struggles and been bound by a deep sense of class solidarity. But even they would refuse to give a serious answer. "*Aiyah*, you don't even know how to do that?" they'd repeat, with an over-the-top laugh, making me guess or saying something outlandish for their own amusement.

The only way of getting a proper answer, were I really set on one, was to shoot the breeze with them and waste a lot of time. I didn't have that kind of patience. If they didn't want to help, then they could do it themselves. I also didn't have the same aspirations to learn the trade that they clearly did—they often took pictures of the recipes and methods on their cell phones, whereas I was only there because it was a job. A job I'd had recommended to me by the kind woman in HR, and not one I sought out myself.

Soon enough, I simply stopped asking questions. I couldn't bear my colleagues' embarrassing displays. Selflessness might be a noble virtue, but I suppose it isn't fundamental to being human.

I also didn't have the energy for working on professional relationships. I was no good at it. I just wanted to keep things as simple as possible—the simpler, the better. Not because I felt hurt or upset, just because it was easier.

I was older than them all, anyway; it was right that I try to be understanding of their positions. What's more, I did get along with them. We worked together mostly without problems or arguments, and often hung out after work, going for team dinners or to the community fitness center or Tuanshan Park.

After more than half a year in Xiaguan, my mental health had improved significantly. The friend I'd gone there with left after three months. In 2013, I followed suit, moving to Shanghai where I worked for the next year and a bit. I wrote about this time, and my fourteenth job, in an earlier chapter. I hadn't been to Shanghai before, even though my mom was born there and lived in the city until she was six. Her father was from Changzhou, and her mother from Suzhou. They taught me and my sister Shanghainese when we were children, though they spoke it with an accent. My mom didn't have the standard pronunciation down either, having left so young and not gone back to the city. So, when I got there, I spoke in only Mandarin. One day, a colleague heard me on the phone with my mom and said I sounded like one of the "new Shanghainese." I'm not sure who he meant by that.

In 2014, I quit my Shanghai job and returned to Xiaguan. This time, instead of Ninghe Lane off Longxi Road, I stayed on the north side of the Xi'er River in Upper Guanyi Village. My plan, initially, was to run a small business or two. I had a few dozen thousand in savings, and the editor who had gone to D City with me to start an automobile magazine had expressed interest in partnering again. We were going to open a store that sold imported snacks, which I would operate while the editor sourced and mailed products from Guangzhou. When I was there before, Xiaguan hadn't had a store like that, but now there were multiple, and none of them were doing well. When I couldn't find a suitable storefront, I gave up on the idea.

I opted, instead, for a portable stall, which I set up in different spots around Dali University's Xiaguan campus. I paid 150 yuan per month to the city for the privilege. In return, I received a penalty notice, which would serve as my vendor's license.

I sold cute and novelty stationary I bought on Taobao for anywhere from a few yuan to thirty per item. The most I made in a day was around fifty yuan; on days it rained, I made nothing. City management officers often got in the way of me even setting up, with excuses like there being some government leader visiting tomorrow, so I should keep away for the next week. I didn't earn enough doing it to risk punishment, so I only opened, intermittently, when I could. They didn't refund me for lost business, of course, and I had no way of chasing them up, since I had ostensibly paid a fine, not rent. But I wasn't going to lose sleep over this. I would stay open for a couple hours around midday, then another three or four in the evenings.

I started writing again sometime along the way. I was already reading much more than I had been, broadening my horizons, and had dropped the naïve aspiration of emulating Kafka or Joyce. I stuck to short pieces, mostly, maybe as a result of the switch to using my cell phone, and moved away from writing realist stories. I also picked up the guitar again, buying one cheap on Taobao. It had been ten years since I last played, back when I was still in Beijing. My Shanghai colleagues had also given me a pair of ASICS running sneakers and a Bryton sports watch as going-away presents. So, I kept up the jogging regimen I'd started in Shanghai, making use of the fountain square by the fitness center. My best month, I ran a total of 152 miles.

The landlord at my new place was an elderly Bai woman who couldn't speak Mandarin but really enjoyed chatting. She wouldn't let me go without a quick tongue wag whenever she saw me. Yet, in the year-plus that I knew her, I didn't understand a single sentence she said. I just smiled at whatever came out of her mouth. She talked, I smiled, and it would eventually make her laugh.

I didn't work a day that I lived in Upper Guanyi Village, and it was a magical year. I never got the feeling time was passing me by, because I was living each day conscientiously, which meant it always had significance. Had Alexander the Great happened to ask me what I wanted then, I, like the philosopher Diogenes, would have told him, "Don't block my light."

Yet, at the same time, I had seriously negative thoughts going around my head. I wasn't depressed, that I knew for sure. I just didn't enjoy being around people. I have been sharing my work experiences here, and it's difficult, doing that, not to touch upon other sides of life. They are all so intertwined that to only talk about one part of the whole experience runs the risk of misleading readers. But there are things I am willing to share, and some things I don't want to, so I suppose it's a risk I'm taking. A person can be both very optimistic and pessimistic at once; this isn't a contradiction. People's mindsets are complex, even polyphonic; there can be multiple melodies all playing over the top of each other. I am not interested in analyzing what caused my mindset back then, and I don't necessarily think I could. But I looked through my journal from that period and found an entry that I am comfortable sharing, and that maybe could work as a side-on perspective for reflection on it. The title is "After the Sun Goes Down":

> *Sometimes, it is as if all joy saves itself for night. Even after the sun goes down, and the temperature plummets, throwing on a windbreaker and pulling a hat on tight before setting out is enough to forget the cold. At the square, by the water, the children let off firecrackers. They chase after one another, beneath the glimmering night sky, roughhousing and laughing. There is so much happiness that the darker sides of life and human nature seem too far away to ever impinge on our joy. Returning home for a nightcap only deepens this feeling.*
>
> *But drinking and firecrackers are for the evening alone. In the day, we still have to face reality, that nonsensical*

brute as strong as an ox, that always manages to prove itself right in the end. Whosoever dares question it is asking for trouble.

Saying one must accept reality is just another way of asking reality to accept oneself. Claiming to reject reality is just another way of saying one has been rejected by it. We mustn't let false victories fool us. In the face of reality, it is best to forget about "winning" at all. But what can we say about reality without sounding naïve, deceiving ourselves, or inviting scrutiny? Better to say as little as possible. Or better yet, keep one's mouth shut and say nothing at all.

If I trip on a rock, I'll get up again and right myself, dust my clothes off and keep on going. Then, it is the rock that looks absurd. Sitting alone for tens of thousands of years, reflecting on the unnecessary and trivial suffering it caused, it will ultimately attain enlightenment and learn to be kind to the world.

Artists often seek refuge in spiritual purity—what they are, they strive to become more so, sometimes to an unimaginable, even bewildering and frightening, extent. Yet, if they cannot achieve that level of purity, the world in their eyes will lose its sheen, and their instinct for creation will vanish. So, in a way, Ernst Gombrich was right: There is no such thing as art, only artists.

Since I was back in Dali, I was meeting up with my old bakery colleagues again, who were now working in production for an online seller of the local flower cakes. The production workshop was in Lower Guanyi Village, right by Upper Guanyi Village. One of the former sous-chefs—now the "foreman" at the flower-cake workshop—told me he planned to get married and leave the job to move to where his wife was from and open a bakery of his own. He asked if I would go with him. He was from Eryuan County, and his wife's family home was in Binchuan County. So, we traveled to Binchuan twice to do reconnaissance, not in the county seat, but in Binju Town, twelve miles from there. His teacher wife had just been transferred to a nearby school, so they were putting down roots in the village. On a map, Xiaguan to Binju doesn't seem all that far, but they are separated by a mountain range with no direct road between them. We had to go all the way around the mountains, first taking a minibus from Xiaguan to Binchuan, then changing to a country bus to Binju. The first time we took the minibus, I wrote about the scenes inside and how I felt on the journey. This is probably a more vivid and accurate depiction of that moment in time than anything I could produce now, so I've included it here. It's untitled:

There is no need to move to the countryside, it's said, because you can be just as isolated in a city. Distance is a matter of the mind.

Yet, I am sitting on a bus headed into the country, preparing to move here in the near future.

After clear skies for days, today it rained. Tomorrow, the blue skies are forecast to return. A squall like this is a steamed bun nestled among a tray of juicy, fragrant meat dumplings, there to cleanse our spoiled palate after so much overindulgence and keep us sensitive to flavor.

Everyone on the bus is in high spirits. The new year is approaching, and soon they will be reuniting with their loved ones, after a long while apart, and enjoying a sumptuous feast together.

Moments ago, the bus was bouncing cheerfully along the winding mountain roads, and my friend and I, maybe caught up in the festive atmosphere, launched into a spirited discussion: Is this warm, welcoming world a fortuitous inevitability, or an inevitable fortuity?

When neither of us could convince the other that they were wrong, we happily agreed to disagree.

A few migrant workers in the seats in front then caught my attention. Since they had gotten on, they had been chatting loudly and cracking sunflower seeds nonstop. They had scattered the discarded shells all over the floor, as if there weren't a trash bin right next to them. The driver, before starting the bus, gave them only an indifferent look. He seemed numbed to people doing whatever they want, without concern for others. He wasn't going to waste his breath trying to correct them.

From the snatches of conversation I could make out, I knew the workers hadn't received their full wages. They had worked a year in the city, on the meagerest of monthly allowances, and now that the project was complete, the money they were rightfully owed was nowhere to be seen. It wasn't hard to imagine the awkward bind they would face when they arrived home for the new year empty-handed. Yet, none of them were being particularly woeful or angry. Their eyes were bright and sparkly, and their voices full of strength and conviction. They were locked in a debate about distributive justice and fair social allotment, passionately, if crudely, comparing the merits and drawbacks of reformism versus revolution in advancing society. They spoke of the future with eager anticipation, impatient for the Spring Festival to pass so they could return to the construction sites they longed for and continue to lay the foundations for their happiness.

Seeing these positive attitudes of theirs, I couldn't help but reflect that there might be some truth to the saying "Ignorance is bliss." Though I do know some remarkable individuals who never let their considerable knowledge weigh them down. They navigate through it like seasoned sailors negotiating hidden reefs, mapping principles in their minds so as to never have one unexpectedly interfere with the simple joys of life. Such exceptional people are the direct reason why the total sum happiness of society has significantly increased.

We are fortunate to live in the greatest era in human history, one in which our historical duty is not to struggle against scarcity, ignorance, and pointless suffering as our predecessors did. Our duty is to boldly embrace happiness. The alternative is a crying shame.

If I wasn't sitting on this bus, I would be on my feet singing in praise of life, of the world, of this magnificent age!

This was actually the result of a writing exercise. Although hyperbolic and partly made-up—and also a tad satirical—the carefree optimism and elation it conveys were really what I felt at that time.

My Fifteenth Job

We started preparations in the run-up to the Spring Festival in 2015. After months of back-and-forth discussions and scoping out Binju Town, we finally put our plan into action: the former sous-chef rented a storefront for his bakery, and sublet me a portion of the space to run as a deli. We shared the rent, to reduce the pressure on each of us and make it possible to bail the other out if necessary. The sign and interior refurbishment were done by contractors from the larger Binchuan. I sourced stainless steel workbenches and storage shelves, as well as a refrigerated deli counter and a cup-sealing machine, from a market in Xiaguan. Then on JD.com, I bought a 228-liter chest freezer and two portable induction cooktops.

Applying for the business license, I realized my ID had expired and, if I wanted to renew it, I had to return to the region where I was registered as a resident. That was a long way to travel, so I just went ahead without one. My partner had a license for the bakery, anyway, and we were essentially a single business since we shared the same unit. The government also had a new policy: Small businesses paid no tax if their monthly revenue was less than a hundred thousand yuan. So, I wasn't evading tax.

Still, there remained the tricky issue of accommodation. Binju had no workers from out of town and so no rooms for rent. It took some serious searching to find a farmhouse, opposite the health center, which I was allowed to stay in for 1,200 yuan for the year. Our bakery and deli opened for business in April 2015. Discounting the stall in Xiaguan, this was my fifteenth job.

We were located on New Street in the town center, which consisted of little more than two parallel streets and another street that dissected them, with a clear view from one end to the other. The staff in the two-story supermarket were young women, all around twenty years old, who seemed to be from the nearby villages. My store hadn't been open a week before these women started visiting, not to buy anything, but full of questions that they asked, giggling, with their hands over their mouths. Some came in groups, laughing and teasing each other, while those who came alone were hesitant and sheepish. They had no interest in what I was selling. This bemused me at first, but I soon cottoned on to what they were doing: They were young women without husbands, and I was the new guy in town. They were showing their faces, in case I shared their intentions and we could start talking. The giveaway was they didn't set foot in my colleague's bakery. But he was already married. This way of seeking out prospective partners was new to me, and felt very Jane Austen—though I'm no aristocrat and have no estate. But after realizing I wasn't interested, they never came again. When we passed each other in the supermarket, as far as they were concerned, I was just another customer.

Binju is in a remote area and had a sparse, scattered population whose lives revolved around agriculture. Very few people moved there for work. There was a market once a week, which brought local villagers into town, but they had only so much money to spend. There were very few development prospects. But that wasn't what I was there for. I was born in Guangzhou, and had worked in Shanghai and done business in Nanning, the provincial capital of Guangxi—all these places with apparently unlimited potential for development, yet I seemed to have gotten nowhere. Development didn't suit me, it turned out. Rural life, meanwhile, offered so much that was novel and interesting, and right then I wanted to give it a try. Maybe the reason things hadn't gone my way in the past was because I had been in the wrong place. Besides, Binju's scenery alone had a real draw for me. I thought that if I could just make the deli profitable, I would hire a young worker to free up half my time for writing, and then I could stay there long-term. This didn't sound all that difficult to do, but I was sadly mistaken.

I mainly sold two types of products at the deli: drinks and *lou mei* food. The *lou mei* was mostly various soy-braised offcuts of duck and vegetarian bites and occasionally included pickled chili peanuts and chicken claws. But there was no duck for sale in Binju, and lotus root was difficult to come by. So I bought a secondhand electric bike for riding into the county seat once or twice a week to restock. The drinks ingredients I ordered on Taobao. They were powder pouches and liquid concentrate for making bubble tea and fruit juices. I also slow cooked honeydew sago, a sour prune and osmanthus drink, and soups made of mung beans and snow fungus with lotus seeds, as well as other sweet beverages. "Cold Shrimp"—frozen rice milk drops in brown sugar water—had been the only sugary beverage sold in Binju until then, at 1.5 yuan a bowl.

My products were what Binju had been missing, was how I saw it, but the business never took off. The *lou mei* bites I sold were more like fast food than meals, and the locals seemed to have zero interest. Maybe the desire for fast food comes *after* material comfort, or when some light relief is needed from the pressures of living. Either way, the people of Binju apparently didn't qualify.

The vegetable market did already have a street food stall, which might have been part of the problem. It was in a better location than mine, so there was no point in me trying to compete. Plus, I would have struggled to keep doing the sweet beverages, when I made about as much from them as the food, and the drinks were easier to make.

Purely selling drinks was also out of the question. There were two stores that did that already, not far from me, both of them bigger, and with tables and chairs, and snacks for sale. Customers could sit there and chat and play cards. Whereas I had a couple dozen square feet to work in and could only sell takeout. This worked to my advantage only because I could undercut the others on price. But again, not enough locals bought takeout for me to get by on drinks sales alone.

I shared a rundown of my day on WeChat on June 6, 2015. It's the only reason I can still remember how an average day at work went back then. All of the tasks were so trivial. I've neatened the post up a little, but this is mostly how it looked originally.

> 8 AM—Got out of bed and straight away took out the duck and vegetables I left in the stock overnight. Boiled the stock then added them again to simmer for twenty minutes, then turned off the heat and let them sit. Washed the duck intestines left to defrost overnight, then blanched and cut them into pieces, before placing into the stock off the heat. (Duck intestines should only be left to sit in the stock, not boiled.)
>
> 9:30 AM—Drove to the county seat and purchased 22 lb. duck legs, 26 lb. duck neck, 8 lb. duck intestines, 2 lb. duck feet, and 11 lb. lotus root, as well as various other ingredients.

11 AM—Returned to shop. Removed foods from the stock, and put on display. Opened the store. Boiled tapioca pearls for the bubble tea, and mixed the ingredients for the lemon water. Boiled the sweet drinks and soups.

1 PM—Defrosted the raw duck ingredients. Prepared the lotus slices, shelled eggs, kelp knots, and tofu skin.

3 PM—Washed the raw duck ingredients, blanched in water, then put them to soak in room-temperature stock along with vegetables, eggs, and tofu.

4 PM—Boiled a new pot of the sold-out sour prune and osmanthus drink.

5 PM—Removed the recently soaked duck and vegetables from the stock, then heated the stock to a boil and returned the ingredients to it for twenty minutes, before leaving to soak for longer off the heat.

6:30 PM—Removed duck and vegetables from the stock, for cooling and blow-drying with a fan, then put them in the deli display.

8:30 PM—Defrosted raw duck ingredients. Prepared vegetables and vegetarian foods.

10 PM—Washed and blanched the defrosted duck, before leaving to soak in stock along with vegetables at room temperature.

11 PM—Closed the shop. Put the remaining food in the freezer. Filled the ice trays. Cleaned down the store

surfaces and utensils. Disinfected the restroom and took out the trash.

00:15 AM—Went back to my room, showered, and washed clothes.

01:15 AM—Returned to the store.

01:45 AM—Slept in the store.

I underestimated how much ice I would need, early on. The milk teas and fruit juices were made to order, with a ratio of one part hot water to three parts ice in every cup. After a good shake, this came out to three parts liquid to one part ice. I had no ice machine, so this meant putting a lot of ice trays in the freezer, and to leave space for those, I had to limit the amount of duck ingredients I kept in stock at any one time. So, I would buy less, but have to restock more often—once or twice a week.

I went into town on the day I recorded, or else I would have opened at around half past nine.

For the *lou mei* meats, I made one pot in the mornings and another in the afternoons. Any fewer, and the food would dry up from sitting in the display cabinet for too long and become chewy.

At night, I slept on a mattress on the store floor, because the room I was renting was in a simple prefab structure, with a thin roof and no insulation. The summer sun beating down on it all day long turned it into an oven, and I couldn't sleep no matter how hard I tried. But the summer also brought with it insects, which were unavoidable even in the store.

Out the back there was an alley with a field beyond it, which was the same for the store on the other side. The crop in both fields, when I first opened, was soybean, which after the harvest was rotated for sweet corn. A pound of soybeans sold for 0.8 yuan at the local market, and the sweet corn for some equally low price I've forgotten. All I'm saying is that the fields produced very little profit, but they were a source of countless bugs. Longhorn, stag, and dung beetles and many other kinds I had never seen in the city, and rarely in Xiaguan, were crawling and buzzing around my store daily. And all kinds of locusts, too—dozens of species, if you were able to check, I imagine. But most terrifying of all were the termites, which swarmed in the thousands and got into everything. Of course, I was stuck with my lights on, so people could see I was open. On particularly bad evenings, I was forced to close early because the termites had covered me head to toe and wouldn't be swatted away. I couldn't touch the deli counter door without them flying straight in. It made doing business impossible.

But besides all the nuisances that came with the summer there, at least it boosted the sales of cold drinks. As soon as temperatures started to fall with the arrival of autumn, the refreshing and sweet beverages became harder and harder to sell. The same went for the *lou mei*, though the impact was small by comparison.

It was at this time that my former editor, who had said he wanted to go into the snack shack business with me, got in touch about running an online store together in Guangzhou. He was very persistent, calling and messaging every day, breaking down the pros and cons, laying out our future. Meanwhile, the Binju store had hit a rough patch, and I was struggling to envision many alternatives for running it, given how small the space was. I also had no plan for the coming winter. I was in a real quandary. One major block was that Binju was far from the sort of place that could change overnight, and a population of that size was hardly going to create any significant growth in the near future. It all meant that the obstacles I faced today would be same the obstacles I faced tomorrow. I was working fifteen-, sixteen-hour days, without any time to read; if the business could do no more than hang on by a thread, with no lifeline in sight, it really wasn't a long-term proposition. I weighed up my options and eventually decided to leave. Having talked it over with my baker colleague, I moved to Guangzhou at the end of 2015.

My Sixteenth Job to My Nineteenth

My former editor had already been out of the media industry for some time, having joined a partnership in a factory for rear-view car cameras, in which he became a small shareholder. But rising staff costs and ever more intense competition had hamstrung the business, and he and an equal shareholder had started looking for ways out. For the webstore he was proposing, he tapped me and another colleague from our comic book days who was now his lover. He didn't tell me this until I moved back to Guangzhou.

This time, the editor was the major stakeholder, and our colleague and I each owned only small shares in the company. The three of us were throwing our lots in together again, more than a decade after we last tried this. It would be my sixteenth job. We survived for eighteen months.

Although it was less than a year in when I started itching to leave, I persevered for fear of hurting their feelings and spent the rest of my time with the company just about passively coping.

I stayed in the camera factory's accommodation, with one other person, in a room that could have fit eight. When the factory couldn't keep up with orders, we would lend a hand on the production line.

The editor had become obsessed with a podcast about innovation, hosted by Luo Zhenyu. Luogic TalkShow was its name, and it was very popular at the time. He enthused enough over the podcast and Luo that I gave it a listen, but it did nothing for me besides put me off. Luo Zhenyu worked in culture, the editor claimed; if I wanted to write, I should pay attention to the guy.

Yet, all I saw was a salesperson, a businessman. The fact he sold books or was, apparently, a "hero of culture" didn't change this.

It was the way he went about selling the books, more than anything: Customers didn't find out the title they were spending their money on until they received it in the post. He would sell twenty to thirty thousand copies of a neglected history book like this, at full price. This was shocking to me, not impressive. People weren't really buying the books to read them. That's at least how it sounded. Their motive was doubtful, anyway.

But the editor worshipped Luo Zhenyu. So much so, he was starting to sound like him. Back in Yunnan, I had been blissfully unaware that such a person even existed, so of course I didn't recognize the editor's newfound confidence and enthusiasm as anything other than genuine excitement at a promising new opportunity.

He also insisted I read a number of best-selling books he owned on business and innovation. I obliged, and though the foreign authors wrote okay, the Chinese writers were terrible. These were titles he believed would benefit my writing, since he believed there were universal principles that underly all things. I had been at it for years and still seen no success, he explained; I had to start rethinking my approach. He wasn't wrong, but I knew what he meant by success, and what I actually needed to work on was not what he had in mind. Then, chatting one day, he remarked that I am an overly emotional person. He was wrong, I told him, I'm more rational than most other people are. But this only made him laugh, as he said I was talking nonsense. It occurred to me then that he was conflating rationality with utilitarian pragmatism (with none of the negative connotation). He believed that anything other than a utilitarian approach to life was irrational. It was strange to think that ten years earlier, when we were both still in our twenties, we hadn't been all that different as people. But I knew his heart was in the right place. He already did all he could for me, even though he wasn't in the best financial situation himself. In his view, I was his trusted coworker, a longtime friend; no matter how disparate our values, he felt I was someone he could safely bank on and not have to worry. In my view, the people he ought to be worried about were those whose values most closely resembled his own.

He had made it clear at the outset that what he wanted to create was not just a webstore, but a cultural brand, for which the store was simply our launchpad. But because he'd proclaimed Luo Zhenyu a man of culture, I was no longer so sure. After registering the company, we opened a business on Taobao under its name. The alternative, Tmall, had temporarily stopped offering the type of account we intended to apply for, and the investment threshold was too high there, anyway. We planned to build from the bottom up, slowly, while acquiring more experience. Our main product was car air fresheners, which we initially sourced from wholesale markets, before moving towards adding our own logo at a factory, then finally designing and producing them ourselves. This was the plan the editor had long been set on, regardless of whether I joined him or not.

But by 2016, Taobao's traffic had reached its peak, and it was unlikely that the number of active users was going to grow significantly. The platform's way forward was to increase the average spend per customer, elevating individual-user consumption to the next level. For a medium-to-small business like us, this meant it became harder and harder for our store to get free traffic—we either had to drive traffic from elsewhere or pay for boosts.

The reality was a business of our size was more suited to a platform like Pinduoduo. Only, none of us had used Pinduoduo before and we all shared the preconceived notion that the site was solely for selling low-end goods. Our product was mid to high range, insisted the editor, and if we had our sights set on TMall, we should stick to the Alibaba ecosystem and learn its ins and outs. So, we put all our energy into researching how to gain traffic for free, and ended up simply wasting time. We couldn't see the bigger trend for our own theory that optimization was how to build traffic, and we would be okay if we only kept on refining. This being the editor's first online store, he had very little idea how to run one, but he was a fast learner and much more invested than I was. We scoured the internet for instructional videos, listened to countless lectures, asked ourselves repeatedly what we were doing wrong, and eventually resorted to reading article after article on Paidai123. Disappointingly, all we found there were self-congratulatory puff pieces that skirted any talk of key operations and cast minor factors as if they were actually what mattered, seemingly to suggest that the authors had managed things nobody else could. Realistically, most breakout sales successes were driven by data generated in advance, not the other way around. Opening a business or personal store on Taobao might have seemed cheap on the surface, but there were hidden costs at every step if you wanted to get clicks. Alibaba isn't a charity, after all. You even had to spend money to be able to gather sales data, so you would know where better to spend your money in the future. There really is no such thing as a free lunch.

But even with data, spending money is an art. It requires a certain technique, or else you risk it going down the drain. This is obvious with paid ads, but less so for another popular method of sales manipulation from back then: assigning hidden coupons for products and having Taobao affiliates post them in discount groups, to attract orders at extremely low prices, with the affiliates earning commission on every purchase made. This way of generating initial sales was much safer and more efficient than relying on fake orders, which became hugely risky if done to excess—a single one might cost over ten yuan on some more secure platforms. Sales from discount groups were at least real, even if they were pricey for the seller. Whether that money was earned back depended on the after-sales data. We tried manipulating the numbers like this for several products, but too many orders had issues, which made the data look bad, and the products dropped quickly down the search engine ranking. In the end, we couldn't even cover our initial investments.

I had lived a frugal and hard-up life for long enough by then that I had developed something of a peasant mentality, resistant to spending money. If ever, over the years, my savings had fallen below ten thousand yuan, I would start to fret. That was my mental yardstick for safety. So, forced to spend money, I didn't know what to do. I mean, when it came to business, I was passive and conservative. I wasn't thinking about how to move things forward—the next step. My concern was how to avoid bankruptcy. And the answer was simple: Spend less.

Perhaps noticing this about me, my two partners began to frequently propose their own ideas. Officially, I was the one in charge of running the webstore, but in practice, any decisions were made between the three of us. Not that either of them had real business management experience to contribute. The editor, as invested as he was, struggled to grasp the basics early on, and wasted a lot of time dragging us into discussions about insignificant points and even making wrong calls. We should have given more time to selecting our products, but I wasn't going to suggest this in case I was the one who had to interact with the wholesalers. Anyway, the next part of the plan was to stick our own branding on products and, all being well, build a strong partnership with a single factory, so this was my excuse for not widening the search for new products and suppliers.

But even if we found the right product, we would still have to spend money to make it sell. Taobao provided exposure based on various user feedback metrics, so new products naturally received limited visibility, and their feedback data was prone to randomness. Meanwhile, the competition would be "maintaining" their data ("maintaining" being a euphemism for "manipulating"), so if we didn't hurry to match them, the product would struggle to gain traction. And similarly, if we ever achieved steady sales and managed to accumulate more data, the moment we let things slip, it would feel like being back to square one. The only way to make sure Taobao would keep directing traffic your way was to keep your data consistently strong.

This was complicated by the platform's review system. On Tmall, customers only rated businesses and products out of five stars; on Taobao, they also gave a rating of good, average, or bad. It was another data point for us to have to throw money at and, if you ask me, the most exhausting one to sustain. In order to save money in the early days, I chose not to outsource the task and would contact any customers who gave average or bad reviews myself. Just making those daily calls alone was enough to give me a stomachache.

By the end of 2016, I was certain this wasn't the right job for me; it was making me unhappy, so I told the others I was going to leave. But the editor and I had a conversation about responsibility, and hope, and his vision for the future, and he gently twisted my arm into staying.

It would be months later, in May 2017, that I finally parted ways with them as I'd wished.

After leaving the online business, I didn't have another moment to waste. My savings were running low. Within a few days, I found a new job through 58.com. This was at D Company, which I wrote about earlier in the book—my seventeenth job. There, I worked permanent night shifts, my schedule turned upside down. The silver lining was that the long hours and isolated location meant I had very few opportunities to spend money, which made it easier to save. Objectively speaking, the job was definitely tough—twelve hours of lifting and hauling heavy goods, nonstop, with barely a bite to eat for most of it. But I'd say that this work was in my "comfort zone." Sometimes, when the exhaustion became unbearable (or, more like, I couldn't fight the drowsiness any longer), I let my mind drift back to the year I spent in Upper Guanyi Village, reliving it in snatches. They gave me warmth, those memories, and returned my strength.

I resigned almost a year later, in March 2018, and moved to Beijing. There, I delivered parcels for S Company for six months, then for Pinjun Express for a further fourteen. In December 2019, Pinjun Express ceased operating, and my colleagues and I were let go. These were my eighteenth and nineteenth jobs.

Conclusion

Back in my Shanghai days, I met up, in person, with two friends from the literary forum. As we ate, we took turns reading aloud from short pieces we liked. It wasn't until I sat down to write about those times that this memory even came back to me. We met in People's Square, where we browsed a two-story bookstore, and I bought *A Sportsman's Sketches* by Ivan Turgenev.

The piece I read for my friends that day seems to me an ideal way to end this chapter. I chose to share some prose from

Virginia Woolf's *The Common Reader*. Woolf appears to have loved reading biographies, many of them about famous figures but also some about more ordinary folk. This piece was her response to the *Memoirs of Mrs. Pilkington*.

I couldn't find any information about the book itself online. Maybe the author really was that unknown. Mrs. Pilkington—or rather Ms. Laetitia, since Pilkington abandoned her—was from a declining aristocratic family in eighteenth-century Britain. She was born around half a century before Jane Austen. An educated woman, she inherited no wealth and was deserted by her husband to raise their two children alone. She made her living writing, which explains the memoirs, but her bread and butter were stories about the underbelly of the upper classes. She claimed she would write anything for money, so it is no surprise that her work hasn't really endured. If it hadn't been for Woolf, I would never have known she existed. This great-granddaughter of the Earl of Kilmallock, who lodged alongside the footmen and laundresses of the dukes she once mixed with, would eventually end up in jail for rent arrears. And yet this barely scratches the surface of her many "wanderings"—or "failings."

Laetitia prayed (only to find herself locked in Westminster Abbey by mistake), begged (and was humiliated, at least that's how she saw it), contemplated suicide—twice. But she also possessed an immense passion for life; she loved and hated with unrelenting ferocity. She viciously cursed out anyone who hurt her and made mockeries of them in her scurrilous stories (taking creative license where it pleased her); and this very same woman cherished the meal of plover's eggs she once shared with her tutor, and every wink of sleep she managed in spite of buzzing mayflies.

She was both emotional and thick-skinned, it seems. She had a natural, dramatic flair to her feelings and, in her writing, an instinct to "give pleasure," which cast the hardship she suffered less as a cruel fate and more like tragicomedy fit for the stage. Her resilience brought her back from adversity on repeated occasions, so she could throw herself once more into life with all her signature brio intact—her infectious love and hate as strong as ever. A lady of refinement, with a salty side, she was both compassionate and vengeful. The first time I read this portrait of her, I was moved to tears. Woolf concludes it with these words:

> All had been bitterness and struggle, except that she had loved Shakespeare, known Swift, and kept through all the shifts and shades of an adventurous career a gay spirit, something of a lady's breeding, and the gallantry which, at the end of her short life, led her to crack her joke and enjoy her duck with death at her heart and duns at her pillow.
>
> (Virginia Woolf, *The Common Reader* [Harcourt, Brace and company, 1925], 175)

Love amidst despair—this is the light that illuminates life. Though her social status declined, her spirit remained noble and pure. Here, I want to pay tribute to Ms. Laetitia, whose own story has comforted and touched me, and lifted me in times I've felt lost. I dedicate this to her many "failings, which were great."

5

The Other Sides of Life

During my final days at Pinjun Express, when I was finishing my rounds as early as one or two in the afternoon, I would while away the remaining hours at Jingtong Roosevelt Plaza, to take advantage of the air conditioning. I liked to sit in the employee dining area, behind the Acasia Food Court on the basement floor, where delivery drivers waited to pick up orders and took breaks. The mall stacked spare tables and chairs there, as it was a dead end only dimly lit with what little daylight filtered in through the south-facing glass wall. After being under the glaring lights of the shopping area, entering that space was like stepping backstage, with the curtains drawn.

The time I spent back there was very meaningful to me. I will always remember it and how I felt then.

In the quieter hours, delivery drivers would sit there chatting, taking naps, playing or scrolling on their cell phones . . . and I sat by them, earbuds in, listening to music and observing. I had nothing else going on. I tried to imagine their lives.

Like me, most of them wouldn't settle down in Beijing. Their days as drifters in the city were numbered, just one part of the long expanse of the rest. So, what about the other parts? They invested their every moment in Beijing into earning money, and it is no great mystery how hard that is. But what was it that drove them to do this, made them willing to sacrifice so much? Maybe the answer varied from person to person. But, supposing work is something we are compelled to do, a concession of our personal will, then the other parts of life—those that remain true to our desires, that we choose to pursue, in whatever form they take—might be called freedom.

Freedom was something I rarely thought about when working. I think I had decided it could never be found there, since the two represented opposites. Work meant having to meet demands and expectations, whether of your boss, or clients, or—as I learned when running my own business—of market observations and analysis. It was about being effective to secure compensation.

There are exceptions out there, I'm sure; people who enjoy both the nature and structure of their work so much it aligns, in a way, with what they want to be doing. Or those who, inversely, have gone after their desires and found there is an employer or market that needs them to do just that, which in turn affords them a certain freedom. But this kind of luck is rare. I know a few people whose jobs are undemanding enough that others describe their work as "freedom," though they do so in envious tones. Whether those lucky people themselves agree, only they can say.

My dad's job gave him a lot of "freedom": he used to spend his days on the clock drinking tea and reading the newspaper. His chief responsibilities were buying, managing, and distributing office supplies, and occasionally writing promotional articles that no one ever read. But he has been retired for years, and after endless reforms, his unit is no longer as laid-back as it used to be. Still, I know him well enough that I can confidently say the concept of freedom has never really existed in his mind. If I were to try to discuss it with him, he would probably respond with some tiresome nonsense.

It makes me think that freedom is actually a matter of consciousness, and not of what you possess. A farmworker with little formal education will not consider himself unfree, despite the agricultural calendar dictating the rhythms of his year. During the slack season, he plays cards with family and friends; in the busy season, he finishes a long day of work and returns home in the evenings, takes a drink, and feels content, as if everything he does, he does because he wants to. But the more educated a person, the more complex their thoughts and awareness, the less likely they are to feel free in their work.

So, by freedom, I suppose I am referring to a personal pursuit, of sorts, and self-realization through consciousness of our individual selves—the spiritual essence that differentiates one person from another. If more of us went after this kind of freedom, the world would be a more diverse, more inclusive, more equal, and richer place. It would be all the more colorful. The pursuit of freedom is what shapes our individual trajectories, our personal goals, and stops us from having to vie for space on a single, narrow path. Just as the adaptability of genes to an environment is based on their diversity, the overall wellbeing and happiness of society is based on the spiritual diversity of its people. And as the German philosopher Gotthold Ephraim Lessing said, the pursuit of truth is more valuable than its possession.

Well, the same goes for freedom. Maybe it is something we can strive for but never quite attain, and maybe I will never reach it my whole life, but that doesn't matter. Because the pursuit is more precious than the attainment, and this holds true for every person and for the world as a whole—like our ideals and our convictions, it is the fulcrum of our lives, not their content.

I returned to Beijing from the south after the Spring Festival in 2020. The sudden eruption of the Coronavirus epidemic almost emptied the streets of people for the longest time and left many of the stores I used to frequent shuttered or even closed for good. The feeling was as if the Spring Festival was dragging on, preventing people from resuming their normal lives. Some of my old colleagues had managed to find new jobs, and others were staying with their families, in their hometowns, waiting to see how things would unfold.

We had just received our severance packages from Pinjun Express. I got the equivalent of two and a half months' salary, which arrived in my account at the same time as my last month's pay and the returned five-thousand-yuan deposit. This came out to around thirty thousand yuan in total, which though not a large sum gave me some reassurance, especially when the pandemic made everything so uncertain.

It was over this period that I posted some pieces I wrote online, and one of them, about doing night shifts at D Company, attracted an unexpected amount of attention. Two editors at *instance*, Feng Junhua and Peng Jianbin, reached out after reading it and, when I filled them in on the rest of my work history, suggested I also write about being a courier in Beijing. So I did, and after that I wrote about my experiences in the bike shop in Shanghai. Those things had happened so long ago, but I was finally putting them down in words.

Here is a good place to say something about my life outside of work. I'm not a complete newcomer to writing. From 2009 to mid- 2011, I spent nearly three years at home, without a job, reading and writing. The challenges I faced then, and since, when it comes to writing are complex—involving factors both personal and external. I'm not a naturally talented writer, by any stretch of the imagination, but if there is anything worth taking away from my awareness, concept, or practice of the art, it is only because I have invested so much time and energy into it. In this respect, I'd even say the fact I earned so little from those early published works—far from enough to make a living—was a fortunate thing. It allowed writing to be more personally significant, more special and pure to me. Although I didn't write much at that time, writing has since become one of the other parts of life, a part that belongs to freedom.

It has become one of two states I have alternated between for years now: working and writing. These states were mutually exclusive because the work alone sapped so much of my time and emotion that I only wanted to relax and decompress afterward, not think about anything. Of course, my nature is to blame here: In life and work, I struggle to feel motivated in situations where others receive positive reinforcement; and, at the same time, I create psychological barriers where other people see none. This was why, when I wanted to write, I quit work so I could give my whole focus to it. This intermittent cycle of work and writing has been my lifestyle for almost a decade. Perhaps this is also a form of compromised freedom? I live half my life free of work, and the other half consumed by it.

But that is not to say we shouldn't also look to gain self-affirmation and happiness through the work we do. If we see no value in it, beyond a means to make ends meet, then we are dooming ourselves to a bleak psychological landscape. Maybe this is why the simpler the labor, the more easily I feel positively motivated by it, because I can very directly see the value it brings to others. Like in my last stint as a courier. When I handed over a parcel to a customer, I could see the satisfaction and excitement in their expression, and hear their pleasant thank-yous. I liked how that made me feel—useful—like my labor was useful. This recognition, though not the true drive behind my doing the work, provided the same small happiness I felt when I received my paycheck.

Writing has actually, to some extent, removed the opposition between work and freedom in my life: In the limited choices and more narrow reality, I increasingly feel that many of the ordinary, meaningful moments in life have a much greater influence on the quality of one's existence than various difficulties of reality.

I'm grateful to Pu Zhao, editor at Insight Media, whose encouragement and guidance led me to rewrite, more fully and comprehensively, the first three chapters of this book, and add to them the final chapter to share my remaining work experiences. I fleshed out these accounts with descriptions of working methods, processes, and the workplaces and settings I was in.

This background is crucial to understanding my circumstances and many of the decisions I made at the time.

I am aware that, being central to these experiences rather than a bystander, my narrative inevitably carries with it my own subjective value judgements and perspectives. But were I to filter out these elements, readers would have trouble understanding some of my actions and responses. There are moments where even I cannot say if I have been swayed by my emotions or deviated from objectivity. But I have done my best to shift my perspective and understand the people and events that upset me, and their motives and causes, trying to depict them in as unbiased a way as possible. In fact, today I feel nothing but gratitude and nostalgia for all my experiences with work. I have no lingering anger or resentment—I admit I once did, but I have let it all go. The more I have lived, the clearer it has become that a life filled with hate and anger is not one worth living.